DEVIL'S ADVOCATES

DEVIL'S ADVOCATES is a series of books devoted to exploring the classics of horror cinema. Contributors to the series come from the fields of teaching, academia, journalism and fiction, but all have one thing in common: a passion for the horror film and a desire to share it with the widest possible audience.

'The admirable Devil's Advocates series is not only essential – and fun – reading for the serious horror fan but should be set texts on any genre course.'
Dr Ian Hunter, Reader in Film Studies, De Montfort University, Leicester

'Auteur Publishing's new Devil's Advocates critiques on individual titles... offer bracingly fresh perspectives from passionate writers. The series will perfectly complement the BFI archive volumes.' **Christopher Fowler,** *Independent on Sunday*

'Devil's Advocates has proven itself more than capable of producing impassioned, intelligent analyses of genre cinema... quickly becoming the go-to guys for intelligent, easily digestible film criticism.' *Horror Talk.com*

'Auteur Publishing continue the good work of giving serious critical attention to significant horror films.' *Black Static*

facebook DevilsAdvocatesbooks

DevilsAdBooks

DEVIL'S ADVOCATES

THE BLOOD ON SATAN'S CLAW

DAVID EVANS-POWELL

ACKNOWLEDGEMENTS

I'd like to thank John Atkinson at Auteur for all his help, guidance and support. I'd also like to thank Piers Haggard, Simon Williams and Linda Hayden for being so generous with their time, and the BBFC for their help with materials.

DEDICATION

I'd like to dedicate this book to my amazing husband Simon, who has probably now seen *The Blood on Satan's Claw* more times than is healthy for anyone! Thank you for all your love and kindness.

First published in 2021 by
Auteur, an imprint of
Liverpool University Press,
4 Cambridge Street,
Liverpool
L69 7ZU

Series design: Nikki Hamlett at Cassels Design
Set by Cassels Design www.casselsdesign.co.uk
Printed and bound by CPI Group (UK) Ltd, Croydon CR0 4YY

British Library Cataloguing-in-Publication Data
A catalogue record for this book is available from the British Library

ISBN paperback: 978-1-80034-806-6
ISBN hardback: 978-1-80034-834-9
ISBN epub: 978-1-80034-770-0
ISBN PDF: 978-1-80034-605-5

CONTENTS

SYNOPSIS

A village near London in the early 18th century. Ploughman Ralph Gower (Barry Andrews) unearths a worm-infested, partially decomposed skull from a furrowed field. Frightened, he runs to the nearby manor house, home to Isobel Banham (Avice Landon) and her guest, a visiting Judge (Patrick Wymark). When the Judge accompanies Ralph back to the field, the skull has vanished.

Isobel's nephew Peter Edmonton (Simon Williams) arrives at the manor house, bringing with him his fiancée Rosalind Barton (Tamara Ustinov). Isobel and the Judge do not approve the match and insist that Rosalind sleeps in the long disused attic. During the night something terrifies Rosalind and she screams uncontrollably. The Judge, convinced that Rosalind is mad, has her boarded up inside and arranges for her to be taken to Bedlam. A Doctor (Howard Goorney) arrives to tend to Isobel, who has developed a fever after being scratched by Rosalind. The following day, when Rosalind is collected for Bedlam, Peter sees that her right hand has become a furry claw. Maidservant Ellen Vespers (Charlotte Mitchell) finds the Judge to tell him that Isobel has disappeared in the night from her bed.

While playing in the field with Ellen's children Cathy (Wendy Padbury) and Mark (Robin Davies), Angel Blake (Linda Hayden) discovers something in the soil. Later at Bible class led by the Curate, Reverend Fallowfield (Anthony Ainley), the object is revealed to be a claw. Fallowfield tries to take it from Angel but the children hide it from him.

Under the direction of Squire Middleton (James Hayter) a posse of men are searching for the missing Isobel. That night, Peter is attacked in the attic by a furry, clawed hand. He grabs his knife and hacks at it. The Judge enters to find a crazed Peter cutting off his own hand.

Fearing that an evil force has taken hold of the community, the Judge returns to London with the Doctor's book of witchcraft, intending to study it and promising to return. During his absence he exhorts them to let the evil grow, as it can only be fully defeated once it has manifested.

Two girls approach Mark and lead him through the woodland where there are other children playing in some ruins. Play time turns sinister and culminates in Angel throttling

Mark. Later, his body is found by Ellen in a woodshed. During the night, Angel attempts to seduce Fallowfield, scornfully telling him that his pupils are succumbing to an evil force. Following Mark's funeral, Fallowfield attempts to tell the Squire about Angel, but she accuses him of assaulting her and insinuates that he killed Mark. The Squire has the Curate arrested.

Cathy is accosted by two boys whilst out picking flowers. They lead Cathy through the woods to the ruins where Angel crowns Cathy with May flowers. Led before the partially restored fiend, Cathy has her clothes torn off, exposing the fiendish fur on her back. Cathy is assaulted and raped before being stabbed to death by Angel. Ralph hears Cathy's screams and arrives at the ruins to find her dead body. He returns to the village with her body and tells the Squire that Angel and her followers are behind the killings. The Squire orders Fallowfield to be released.

Peter rides to the Judge's London house, telling him how things have deteriorated in the village. The Judge is ready to return, advising Peter that he will use undreamed of measures to defeat the evil.

Margaret (Michele Dotrice), one of Angel's followers, is rescued by Ralph from being swam as a witch. Taking her to Ellen's house, they discover she has the fiend's fur growing on her thigh, and they call for the Doctor to cut it off. Devoted to the fiend, Margaret flees but she is hunted down and captured by the Judge and his men. Under interrogation, Margaret tells him that Angel and her followers meet in the ruins in the forest.

That evening, the Judge, armed with a cross-shaped sword, leads a mob out across the fields to the woods. The mob arrives at the ruins to find a ceremony in progress and see Ralph entranced and ready to cut the fiend's fur from his leg. The mob attacks and the coven scatter. Angel is impaled upon a pitchfork, and the fiend is run-through by the Judge and heaped upon a fire. The Judge watches as the fiend's body burns.

INTRODUCTION

Mark Gatiss, in the second episode of his and Jonathan Rigby's excellent television documentary series *A History of Horror* (2010) draws together *The Blood on Satan's Claw*, Michael Reeves' *Witchfinder General* (1968) and Robin Hardy's *The Wicker Man* (1973) under the collective moniker of 'folk horror'. This book will not dwell in depth on the folk horror subgenre as, pleasingly, there is an increasing wealth of study here. Alongside the *Folk Horror Revival* series of books, there are two highly recommended surveys of screen folk horror for newcomers: Adam Scovell's *Folk Horror: Hours dreadful and things strange* (2017) and Howard David Ingham's *We Don't Go Back: A watcher's guide to folk horror* (2018). However, the critical role *The Blood on Satan's Claw* has played in the definition of folk horror does need to be addressed before we proceed.

The recent explosion of interest in folk horror, coupled with a continuing appreciation of horror as a reputable film genre worthy of merit and consideration and not simply to be derided and overlooked (itself a fairly recent phenomenon within the wider discipline of film studies), has rehabilitated both *Witchfinder General* and *The Wicker Man*. They have benefitted from re-appraisal following critical mauling upon their original release and now enjoy, not only substantial cult followings, but also critical high regard as two iconic examples of British cinema. Many eminent commentators, academics, and critics, including Robin Wood, David Pirie, Kim Newman, Derek Malcolm, J. Hoberman, Mark Kermode, and the magazines *Total Film*, *Empire*, and *Cinefantastique*, have championed these films over the years, lending expert approval to popular acclaim (not least Ian Cooper's excellent appraisal of *Witchfinder General* (2011) as part of the *Devil's Advocate* range).

While *The Wicker Man* and *Witchfinder General* have stolen the limelight in terms of both contemporary opprobrium and revised appreciation, *The Blood on Satan's Claw* has been much maligned, hidden in the shade of its more celebrated bedfellows. Both on its release, and in subsequent years, *Satan's Claw* has failed to receive a similar apportion of either notoriety or appraisal, at least until *A History of Horror* came along. This is particularly ironic, given that the term 'folk horror' may have originated in direct association with *Satan's Claw*. In April 1970, during the film's production, reporter Rod Cooper from the British trade journal *Kine Weekly*, visited the set and wrote a short report on the film under the title *Folk horror study form Hemdale and Chilton*. It is not clear whether Cooper originated the term or borrowed it from Haggard at the time. By the time director Piers Haggard was interviewed by M.J. Simpson for *Fangoria* magazine decades later, he was comfortable with describing the film as such:

> I grew up on a farm and it's natural for me to use the countryside as symbols or as imagery. As this was a story about people subject to superstitions about living in the woods, the dark poetry of that appealed to me. I was trying to make a folk-horror film, I suppose. (Haggard quoted in Simpson, 2013)

The subsequent Gatiss and Rigby documentary popularised the term, once again through an interview with Haggard. Whether Haggard, Cooper, or indeed someone else either at the time or possibly before, coined the phrase, it is indisputable that it is *The Blood on Satan's Claw* that sits at the heart of this fascinating and ambiguous subgenre. Howard David Ingham acknowledges this: 'it's the only film before about 2008 that was *deliberately* intended to be a folk horror film' (Ingham, 2018: 26 – italics in original).

As Haggard's quotation above indicates, the key concerns of the folk horror subgenre – an attention to the rural landscape, a pre-occupation with the customs and cultures of ordinary people and ordinary communities, the pervasion of dread and the threat of brutality, the continuation or restoration of malign 'old ways' or long-forgotten beliefs – can be traced to *Satan's Claw* and to Haggard's desire to represent an authentically worked and inhabited agricultural landscape, in contrast to the artificial and generic historic mittel-European locales of Hammer's horror output. Since the film's renaissance, Haggard has embraced the term 'folk horror' to distinguish his approach to *Satan's Claw* from the style of the genre's more celebrated antecedents.

The purpose of this book is to add to this critical renaissance of *Blood on Satan's Claw*, and to celebrate a film that deserves a wider popular audience.

PRODUCTION AND RECEPTION

KEY CREATIVES

PIERS HAGGARD OBE, DIRECTOR

Piers Haggard was born on 18 March 1939 to a creative dynasty: his great-great uncle was H Rider Haggard, who wrote numerous works of adventure fiction including *King Solomon's Mines* (1885) and *She: A History of Adventure* (1886), and his father was the actor, writer and poet Stephen Haggard. Despite being born in London, Haggard was raised on a Scottish farm, and his rural upbringing – during which he actively helped with farming and working the land – had a significant influence on his approach to directing in general, and *The Blood on Satan's Claw* in particular.

Haggard started his career in the theatre as an assistant director at the Royal Court in 1960, before moving to the Dundee Rep and Glasgow Citizens Theatres, and then relocating to London as a director for the first National Theatre Company in 1963. It was during his time working at the National that he became familiar with the work of composer Marc Wilkinson, who he would ask to compose the score for *Satan's Claw*.

In 1965 he moved to BBC Television, directing for a variety of programmes including anthology series *Thirty-Minute Theatre* (1965-1973), drama series *Callan* (1967-1972), soap opera *The Newcomers* (1965-1969), and *Armchair Theatre* (1956-1974) for ITV.

In 1966 he had his first experience of feature film work as a dialogue assistant on Michelangelo Antonioni's film *Blow Up* (1966) before making his directorial debut with *I Can't … I Can't* (aka *Wedding Night*) in 1970. The producers of what would become *The Blood on Satan's Claw* had been invited to a screening of *I Can't … I Can't* and, off the back of that, they offered him the directing role. While Haggard was not a typical horror fan, he was an admirer of James Whale's Universal films *Frankenstein* (1931) and *Bride of Frankenstein* (1935), and particularly of Whale's ability to balance the horrific with the poetic and to comment on the human condition. Arguably this attention to human relationships and behaviours is a facet of Haggard's direction that shines through in *Satan's Claw*.

After *Satan's Claw*, Haggard went on to direct the landmark Dennis Potter series *Pennies from Heaven* (1978) for which he won a BAFTA, and the both the television (1979) and feature film (1980) versions of *Quatermass* (aka *The Quatermass Conclusion*). In the 1980s he directed Peter Sellars' last film *The Fiendish Plot of Dr Fu Manchu* (1980) and *Venom* (1982), the latter being a notoriously troubled production where Haggard took over directing from Tobe Hooper. Later he directed an acclaimed television mini-series adaption of Rosamunde Pilcher's *The Shell Seekers* (2006) starring Vanessa Redgrave and Maximilian Schell.

Haggard has been a long-standing campaigner for directors' rights, as President of the Association of Directors and Producers from 1976 and then as Founder and first Chairman of the Directors' Guild of Great Britain, which was founded at Ronnie Scott's Club in London in 1982. He also founded the Directors' and Producers' Rights Society in 1987 and served on its board, and then the board of its successor organisation, Directors UK. Haggard was awarded an OBE in the 2016 New Year Honours for services to film, television and theatre.

ROBERT WYNNE-SIMMONS, SCREENWRITER

Robert Wynne-Simmons was born on 18 August 1947 in Sutton, Surrey. He demonstrated a creative passion from an early age, writing poetry, embarking on writing an opera, and making 8mm films from the age of 12. By the time he left school he had made 15 films, inspired by directors like Antonioni (who Piers Haggard had worked with) and Buñuel, and he had also written plays for the open-air theatre at his school. Wynne-Simmons attended Lancing School in Surrey before studying for an MA in English Literature at Peterhouse College, Cambridge. The College funded the making of Wynn-Simmons' short film *The Judgement of Albion* (1968), a film based on the prophetic writings of William Blake that included the voice talents of Anthony Quayle and Donald Sinden.

His childhood was not entirely a happy one, and he experienced mental and physical bullying from the age of 11 that contributed to intestinal problems from which he nearly died at 19. The sequence in *Satan's Claw* where Margaret undergoes an operation, conducted on the kitchen table in the Vespers' cottage, is directly influenced by two operations he experienced while at Cambridge. His experiences of bullying and illness inspired a number of short stories, and it was these stories that Wynne-Simmons, at the age of 22, drew upon when writing the script for *Satan's Claw*, with its attention to children's horrifying capacity for cruelty.

After *Satan's Claw* Wynne-Simmons worked as a film editor for BBC Television before graduating from the National Film and Television School in Beaconsfield in 1975. He subsequently worked in Ireland for Radio Telefis Eireann, where he directed *Double Piquet* (1979), wrote and directed the multi-award winning *The Outcasts* (1982), and the television drama anthology series *When Reason Sleeps* (1987). In recent years, Wynne-Simmons has turned his attention to composition and theatre work, writing and directing the play *The Deluge*, starring Susannah York, at the Edinburgh Festival in 2006.

DICK BUSH, DIRECTOR OF PHOTOGRAPHY

Dick Bush was a prolific, award winning British cinematographer (winning a BAFTA TV Award in 1967 for *Individual Honour*, receiving a BAFTA nomination for Best Cinematography for *Yanks* in 1980, and a nomination in 1982 for his work on *Victor/Victoria* from the British Society of Cinematographers). Born in Devon on 2 December 1931, Richard Henry 'Dick' Bush attended Plymouth Art College before being called up to serve in the Royal Military Police. After service, he had a variety of jobs, including at Fry's Chocolate and Clark's Shoes, where he produced promotional films. He joined the BBC in 1961 as part of the early outside broadcast team and, from 1968 onwards, worked on films alongside television, with one of his first projects seeing him accompany Malcolm Muggeridge to film in the Holy Land. He worked extensively with director Ken Russell, including on the Omnibus instalment *Song of Summer* (1968), and the films *Mahler* (1974), *Tommy* (1975) and *The Lair of the White Worm* (1988). Bush also worked on some Hammer horror films, most notably the stylish *Twins of Evil* (1971) and, later in his career, with Blake Edwards on a number of the Pink Panther films, including *Trail of the Pink Panther* (1982) and *Curse of the Pink Panther* (1983).

Perhaps his most notable work, certainly for folk horror aficionados and those looking to trace antecedents for his photography for *Satan's Claw*, is his cinematography for

Culloden (1964, dir. David Watkin) and *Whistle and I'll Come to You* (1968, dir. Jonathan Miller). He died on 4 August 1997.

MARC WILKINSON, COMPOSER

Marc Lancelot Wilkinson is an Australian composer and conductor who was born in Paris, France, on 27 July 1929, and who became known for his film scores and his incidental music for the theatre. He studied in the US at Princeton and Columbia Universities, and took private lessons with the French-born composer Edgar Varèse.

Moving to England, Wilkinson became one of the first independent composers to utilise the BBC's new Radiophonic Workshop, following its opening in 1958. He was resident composer and musical director at the RSC, then musical director at the Royal National Theatre from 1963 to 1974, where he composed the scores for Peter Shaffer's *The Royal Hunt of the Sun* (1964) – which is where he met Piers Haggard – and *Equus* (1973), and Tom Stoppard's plays *Rosenrcantz and Guildenstern are Dead* (1967) and *Jumpers* (1972).

He later moved into film scores, composing the music for *...if* (1968, dir. Lindsay Anderson), and the film adaptations of *The Royal Hunt of the Sun* (1969, dir. Irving Lerner) and *Rosencrantz and Guildenstern are Dead* (1990, dir. Tom Stoppard), and music for television, including the incidental scores for the BBC drama mini-series *Days of Hope* (1975), Dennis Potter's *Play for Today* serial *Blue Remembered Hills* (1979), and several episodes of *Tales of the Unexpected* (1979-1988).

Wilkinson's score for *Satan's Claw* has been described as 'easily among the best composed for a British horror film' (Rigby, 2015: 200) and 'some of the finest British horror music ever written' (Ingham, 2018: 26), a heavily modulated English pastoral that queasily manages to be simultaneously playful and unsettling. Haggard and Wilkinson would work together again on the TV series *Quatermass* and its film adaptation *The Qautermass Conclusion*, and *The Fiendish Plot of Dr Fu Manchu*.

Wilkinson continued to influence the aural landscape of 'folk horror' when the makers of *The Wicker Man* asked him to advise composer Paul Giovanni on their film score. Arguably, Wilkinson could be described as the grand architect of folk horror's soundscape. Wilkinson has retired from composition and currently lives in France.

DEVELOPMENT AND SHOOTING

Shortly after graduating from Cambridge University, Robert Wynne-Simmons submitted unsolicited scripts to several film companies. He received a reply from the writer and producer Christopher Neame, who was at the time working with Tigon founder and manager Tony Tenser, in between working for Hammer Studios as an assistant director on *Quatermass and the Pit* (1967, dir. Roy Ward Baker) and *The Devil Rides Out* (1968, dir. Terence Fisher) and as a production manager on *Frankenstein Must be Destroyed* (1969, dir. Terence Fisher). Neame wrote back let him know that Tigon had booked for a film to begin shooting on 1 April 1970; they had received around 30 scripts, none of which they felt was suitable, and were asking Wynne-Simmons for his ideas. Tigon were keen on a portmanteau film, similar to those produced by rival studio Amicus, as it was a format that could be easily adapted into a television series should that be something they wanted to explore:

> Tony wanted three short films because he had some idea that it could be crewed by less technicians if it was short films – which was actually true – with the idea that they could then be assembled together as one film or else marketed separately as support features. (Neame quoted in Hamilton, 2005: 181)

Despite Wynne-Simmons' reservations about the portmanteau concept, within three weeks he completed the first treatment. This script featured multiple storylines, including a young woman driven insane when locked up in the attic by her wicked aunt, a man who is attacked by his own possessed hand and hacks it off, and a group of youths who come across something nasty when out playing in a field. These plotlines were linked by a series of overarching narrative elements: a community gradually infected by an evil that is seeking its restoration, the unearthing of mysterious yet malevolent bones, the notion of the devil taking over parts of people's bodies, and the appearance of a Judge/ magistrate character who would act as the voice of reason and oppose the fiendish goings-on.

This script set the film in the early 19th century during the Age of Steam, and one key scene featured the Judge returning to the village on a steam train. However, Tigon were unhappy with this setting; Neame in particular felt that the Victorian Gothic had been exhausted in horror cinema. Their feeling, following on from the success of *Witchfinder*

General, was that the 17th century was a better fit for a witchcraft theme and that such a topic would seem out of place in the more modern 1800s. Neame and Tenser were also concerned that the ending was too ambiguous and were keen for a far more explicit showdown between good and evil. They also wanted to include a number of elements that they felt would enhance the commercial appeal of the film, again based on the success of *Witchfinder General*, including a Book of Witches (the book that the Doctor owns) and the scene in which Margaret is ducked as a suspected witch. They also wanted the Judge to be cast more as a more definitively heroic character, similar to Peter Cushing's Van Helsing in Hammer's Dracula cycle. To this end, Tigon asked for the Judge to wield a cross at the end of the film when defeating the fiend, something Wynne-Simmons was reluctant to do. The final compromise was for the Judge to have a cross-shaped sword instead.

Initially Christopher Neame, who would go on to be production manager for several Hammer films including *Fear in the Night* (1972, dir. Jimmy Sangster) and *Frankenstein and the Monster from Hell* (1974, dir. Terence Fisher), was to produce the film, however he moved off the project at an early stage. The production of the film was handed on to two independent producers – Peter Andrews and Malcolm Heyworth – who had formed a company called Chilton Films the previous year and who had impressed Tenser. Andrews was a former editor, who had produced children's television shows and travelogues, while Heyworth had previously made short films. They came on board with Andrews focusing on the financial aspects of the project and Heyworth managing the day-to-day production.[1] Tenser only occasionally visited the set during filming.

When the 31-year old Piers Haggard was approached to direct the film it took him by surprise, given his lack of experience with horror cinema. However, the script and the setting, with their focus on the darker aspects of rural life and the notion of a community beset by 'moral and spiritual infestation' (Haggard, 2019), appealed to him. While he had not seen many horror films at the time, he and the crew had an opportunity to watch *Witchfinder General* during the making of *Satan's Claw*, and he was impressed by its sharpness and dynamism. Haggard and Wynne-Simmons developed a rapport and agreed that the anthology approach that Tigon wanted for the film would compromise both on audience experience and commercial yield. Haggard, Heyworth and Andrews eventually convinced Tenser to abandon the anthology concept and focus on one single feature narrative, and Wynne-Simmons, with input from Haggard, set about rewriting the script. This revision is arguably only partially successful, something Wynne-Simmons regrets and attributes to the lack of time available to complete the job. Haggard also noted the difficulties in trying to redraft the anthology script into a single narrative, stating 'ideally, you'd have taken it away for three months and thought it through and structured it better' (Haggard quoted in Taylor, 1996: 93). As such some characters, for example Isobel Banham and Rosalind Barton, disappear from the narrative while the Judge is absent for about half the film. However, while there are some inevitable peculiarities arising from the hasty revisions, they also give the film a pleasingly idiosyncratic character. Mark Morris feels the unconventional progress of the film's production from anthology to single feature 'adds to its sense of queasy and dislocating potency' (Morris, 2019) while Howard David Ingham considers that the film develops, rather appropriately 'like it's a countryside tale, or a series of them, with the narrative flow of gossip' (Ingham, 2018: 27).

Haggard's input was focused on the dialogue; with the change of setting from the 19th to the early 18th century, he tried to make the dialogue more authentically antiquated (Haggard, 2016). In later years he has had mixed feelings over this input, feeling perhaps he was rather over-enthusiastic in doing so, while also pleased that it lends a sense of remoteness and distance to the setting (Taylor, 1996: 93). The focus of this input was with the sequences that wrapped around the key scenes in terms of creating period atmosphere. Haggard was, and has always been, very complimentary about Wynne-Simmon's story, which provided five of so key horror set pieces between which Haggard crafted atmospheric sequences of rurality (Haggard, 2019, audio commentary).

The film had a modest budget of £75,000 (rising to £82,000 by time of release) and an eight-week shoot. The production itself was very smooth with very little in the way of behind-the-scenes drama or complications. The only slight exception to this was Patrick Wymark, who played the lead role of the Judge. Tenser had suggested Peter Cushing or Christopher Lee – Britain's two biggest horror stars of the time – for the role of the Judge, and indeed the part was offered to Cushing, who declined due to the poor health of his wife Helen. Lee was reportedly too expensive for Tigon. Wymark was a star name, having appeared in a number of well-known films, including *Where Eagles Dare* (1968, dir. Brian G Hutton), *Battle of Britain* (1969, dir. Guy Hamilton), and

Cromwell (1970, dir. Ken Hughes), as well as playing Cromwell himself in a cameo role in *Witchfinder General*. Wymark sadly suffered with alcoholism and his drinking was a cause for concern during the shoot. Simon Williams remembers him as 'a fearsome man to spend time with' (Williams, 2019) and 'quite aloof and wasn't particularly warm or friendly' (Williams quoted in Taylor, 1996: 93). Wymark would die of a heart attack in October 1970, shortly after production on *Satan's Claw* was concluded and only three days before opening in an Australian run of Anthony Shaffer's play *Sleuth*. Regardless of behind the scenes behaviour, his performance is crisp with dry wit and a tremendous physical presence; it is not a horror turn, something that Haggard was keen to avoid with all of his cast. Linda Hayden was a casting coup in the role of Angel Blake. She was young at the time of casting, only 17-years-old, and a rising star off the back of her first film *Baby Love* (1968, dir. Alastair Reid), a role that established her as a sex symbol, before then starring in Hammer's *Taste the Blood of Dracula* (1970, dir. Peter Sasdy). Haggard has remarked on his admiration for Hayden and her performance, which is a startling mix of eroticism and menace (Haggard, 2019, *Underneath Satan's Skin*). The cast is exceptionally strong for a horror film, and represents a number of British acting dynasties, including Simon Williams (Peter Edmonton), Michelle Dotrice (Margaret), and Tamara Ustinov (Rosalind Barton).

Wymark aside, the shoot was noted for its general bonhomie, and most of the cast and crew are quick when interviewed to say how much they enjoyed making the film (Williams, 2019; Hayden, 2019). Many were also notable for their youth and this seems to have helped them to bond. Linda Hayden, Tamara Ustinov and Simon Williams have been very complimentary about Haggard and his organisation and management of the shoot (Taylor, 1996; 92). In particular they highlighted his focus on helping the actors to prepare, allowing for a couple of weeks rehearsal time prior to shooting (Hamilton, 2005; 184). Haggard, with his theatre background, put a lot of emphasis on the rehearsal time available, and used it to work with his cast on developing their character relationships. Wynne-Simmons, who was also on hand during filming, has praised Haggard's direction (Taylor, 1996; 92).

There were two substantial changes to the script following its redrafting into a single narrative. Originally the film had a much starker and more brutal ending, involving the Judge enlisting the help of militiamen who indiscriminately killed the villagers in order to eradicate the cult. This far more cynical and nihilsitic ending was changed at Tigon's request. The other change was Cathy's rape. This scene does not appear in the original script; instead it occurs off-screen and her body is found later. Haggard made the decision to feature the rape as a specific scene; as such, the scene shoot was unplanned until the day of filming. Wynne-Simmons recalls that Wendy Padbury, who played Cathy, had not long departed *Doctor Who* (1963-1989, 1996, 2005-) as companion Zoe Heriot and was keen to have a more adult role ('Touching the Devil'). Understandably though, and possibly because of a lack of time to prepare for such a harrowing scene, Ustinov recalls that Padbury found the filming difficult: 'I remember she got very upset ... I think maybe it all went a bit too far' (Ustinov quoted in Taylor, 1993: 93).

Mirroring the relatively smooth nature of the production, the film fared well with the British Board of Film Censorship. Haggard had a good relationship with John Trevelyan, the Secretary to the Board, inviting him to the cutting room to see the edits. Perhaps understandably, the scene that caused the most concern for the censors was the rape. Haggard recalls Trevelyan telling him: 'the thing is Piers, it's sex and violence. You can have sex. That's alright. Violence is alright. But sex and violence, this is what we have to think carefully about' (quoted in Taylor, 1996: 89).

The BBFC records only two reels in which cuts were made: firstly to double reel three, the scene in which Cathy is raped and stabbed; and secondly to double reel five, a scene from the final sequence of the film in which Ralph suggestively fingers a knife while watching a naked coven member (Yvonne Paul) writhing in front of him (BBFC correspondence, 2019). Less then 10 seconds of cuts were made to the film overall (Hamilton, 2005; 200). Additionally, the scene in which a naked Angel attempts to seduce the Curate was optically darkened. Wynne-Simmons recalls another scene that he understood to have been cut:

> There is a scene in the script, which we filmed, where I wanted to show Angel giving oral sex with the 'devil'. It was cut and darkened down but it's still in there, just.
> (Wynne-Simmons quoted in Hamilton, 2005: 200)

The film was passed with the cuts and classified with the new 'X' certificate. Despite the edits, Wynne-Simmons still has mixed feelings about the rape sequence, feeling that the censor's edits, rather than mitigating the impact, instead emphasise it. Rather than the scene being played out directly for the viewer, 'what you have then is a scene with a rape which is largely played out on the faces of the people watching it' (Wynne-Simmons quoted in Taylor, 1996: 93). Instead of expressing censure by focusing on Cathy's distress and horror, the censor's cuts focus on the pleasure the other characters derive from watching the scene.

THE LOCATIONS

The majority of the film was filmed on location in the Oxfordshire village of Bix Bottom, nestled in the Chiltern Hills. A handful of scenes were shot at Pinewood Studios, and a few at other locations nearby including the village of Hurley in Buckinghamshire (for Mark's funeral), the Warburg Nature Reserve and the banks of the Evenlode River (both for some woodland scenes, in particular the scene where Angel confronts Margaret towards the end of the film in the chalk pit), and Hammer's familiar stomping ground of Black Park (for the scene where Margaret is cast into the lake as a suspected witch). Bix Bottom was about half an hour further out from the studio than the production company would have ideally liked, however it presented the best range of locales needed for the film – the farmhouse, the valley, the old church, and a variety of woodland and scrubland – all in close proximity to each other. Haggard certainly feels the film benefits from this range of landscapes; they provide a sense of character to the setting that simply shooting all of it at Black Park would not have fulfilled ('Underneath Satan's Skin'). One of the Bix locations that is of particular interest is the derelict Old Church of St James. This is the ruined building in which the cult meets for its rituals, and where Mark and Cathy are murdered. The film suggests that the ruins are located within the forest, whereas in reality the church is located within fields. The field featured in the pre-credits sequence is located adjacent to the Old Church, as is the road that Peter and Rosalind ride along at the start of the film as they approach the Banham farmhouse. St James' Old Church, most likely built during the 12th century, was the parish church for the former settlement of Bix Brand, a mediaeval village mentioned in the Domesday Book that fell into decline in the 18th century as the village of Bix, one mile to the south, grew in stature. Ultimately the old church was abandoned in 1875 both because of the ongoing costs of repairing the building and because the congregation increasingly favoured the closer St James' Church that was built the previous year in Bix. The roof of the Old Church was removed shortly after its abandonment, the site subsequently falling into an extremely dilapidated state, even being used for animal grazing into the early 20th century. The local community became concerned that the building was in danger of complete destruction – for many years it was on English Heritage's 'at risk' list – and there have been investments from Historic England and the church council to make the building safe, including installing a bench nearby for walkers, and an interpretation board to tell the story of the church's history, as well as making the ruins secure. Some of the more notable features of the Old Church, including some early 16th century stained glass, were rescued for display at the new church. This was not the Old Church's first use as a British horror location; Hammer's Joan Fontaine vehicle *The Witches* (Cyril Frankel, 1966) used it for the coven's lair at the film's dramatic conclusion.

THE TITLE

Wynne-Simmons' script was originally called *The Devil's Skin*. Tigon, however, wanted something different, and several alternatives were considered, including Tony Tenser's favourite (although no one else's) *The Ghouls are Amongst Us*. *The Devil's Skin* continued to be used throughout the shoot, only to be retitled *The Devil's Touch* and then *Satan's Skin* at the end of filming, the title by which the film is known in the USA and other overseas territories (including Sweden and Italy). The title only changed to *The Blood on Satan's Claw* at the very last minute when, following AIP's purchasing the film for distribution, AIP Founder Sam Arkoff thought it was lurid enough to draw crowds (Haggard, 2019, 'Underneath Satan's Skin'). There is no consensus as to whether the film has a definite article or not; consequently the 2010 DVD release is *Blood on Satan's Claw*, while the 2019 Blu-ray release is called *The Blood on Satan's Claw* on the cover, but uses the overseas title *Satan's Skin* during the film's title sequence.

RELEASE AND RECEPTION

The film was released in the US on 14 April 1971 and in the UK on 16 July 1971, before being released to other territories worldwide from November 1971. The film was paired in a double bill with Tigon's *The Beast in the Cellar* (1971, dir. James Kelley) starring Beryl Reid and Dame Flora Robson, a pairing that Haggard did not feel complimented *Satan's Claw*. There was only ever one version of the film sold in all territories; there were no alternative versions created for markets that would expect a film with a greater quantity of sexually explicit material (as was common practice at the time).

It received generally favourable, if somewhat temperate, critical reviews. In *The New York Times*, Vincent Canby said that it was 'cinematic diabolism of some style and intelligence', while Judith Crist said it 'offers a satisfying sense of sunlight-and-terror' (Canby and Crist quoted in Taylor, 1996: 95). The British reviews were less enthusiastic though, with *The Daily Mail* reviewing it as 'as silly as it is repulsive' (quoted in Morris, 2019) while *The Observer* stated that 'it doesn't frighten or convince' (quoted in Hamilton, 2005: 212); there were, however, some positive responses, notably from *Kine Weekly* ('a remarkably successful atmosphere of chilling, supernatural menace') and *The Evening News* ('it comes very near to being a work of art') (both quoted in Hamilton, 2002: 212).

More vociferous, and more surprising (at least certainly to the film makers), was the audience response. Cinema-goers were, at best, indifferent about the film, if not outright hostile. Despite the concerns over the rape scene, more consternation was caused by the scene later in the film in which Michelle Dotrice's Margaret has a patch of fur surgically removed from her thigh. This took Haggard by surprise and he reasoned:

> perhaps because of the lyrical side of it, or the fact that it purports to be real, it attempts to get under your skin. It's not just a sit-back-and-enjoy-it good old horror film ... which possibly made it more disturbing. (Haggard quoted in Taylor, 1996: 95)

Ultimately, the film was not a success at the box office, and Tigon's securing of the large 2,600-seater New Victoria cinema in London's West End proved a mistake; the film was pulled after only a week to be replaced by *Carry on Henry* (1970, dir. Gerald Thomas). The unsettling juxtaposition of the bucolic and the brutal, neatly summed up by Judith Crist's phrase 'sunlight-and-terror', may have confounded audience expectations. The ambiguous ending certainly left some viewers dissatisfied, with Haggard noting in retrospect 'it's my instinct to make things ambiguous, which may be why the film didn't "work" in the marketplace' (ibid.). In many ways Haggard's emphasis on the material and physical historical rural landscape – one that is believable and inhabited – as opposed to the more familiar horror milieu of the time (contemporary Swinging London, Gothic mittel-Europe, or Victorian England) both mark the film out as memorable and different but also arguably limited its appeal. As Haggard has commented, 'I think it fell between two stools. Although there was horror in it, it wasn't a cynical, slightly campy, plenty-of-gore horror film' (ibid.).

Regardless of the lukewarm reception of the film, and notwithstanding the hasty readying of the script for production as a single feature film, both Wynne-Simmons and Haggard are pleased with the final film. In particular Haggard has said:

> for me the film was poetic. One did one's best with the bits that were blatantly commercial, but there were all those other bits that were able to be haunting in a rich way. (Haggard quoted in Taylor, 1996: 89)

Haggard has also reflected that the film is an odd genre piece in that it does not quite fit into any genre; however, he considers that this peculiarity makes for a satisfying and timeless experience (Haggard, 2019, Interview with Piers Haggard).

FANDOM AND LEGACY

The Blood on Satan's Claw was released on VHS in 1993. It was released in 2005 as part of the Tigon DVD Collection, which also included *Witchfinder General*, *The Body Stealers*, *The Haunted House of Horror*, *The Beast in the Cellar*, and *Virgin Witch*, all in a fetching coffin-shaped box. It received an individual film re-release in 2010. A Blu-ray version of the film was first released in 2013, and released again in re-mastered form in 2019. Marc Wilkinson's soundtrack was released on CD and limited edition vinyl LP by Trunk Records in 2007.

The past few years have seen a renaissance for the film, largely thanks to influential enthusiasts like Mark Gatiss, Reece Shearsmith, Matthew Sweet and Jeremy Dyson. Their passionate nostalgia for the film has influenced their own work and they have been vocal champions in bringing the film to ever wider audiences, moving from a cult favourite to mainstream appreciation. In 2018, Audible produced an award winning[2] audio adaptation of the film, starring Gatiss, Shearsmith and Alice Lowe, and featuring Linda Hayden, to great critical acclaim, while a Blu-ray Collector's Edition of the film, complete with a host of new documentaries and interviews including an audio commentary by super-fans Gatiss, Shearsmith and Dyson, was released in 2019.

WHEN IS THE FILM SET?

Commentators, and even the makers of the film, appear undecided as to when the film is meant to be set. Mark Gatiss asserts on the Blu-ray commentary that the film is set in the 1680s, and during his *History of Horror* series he stated that the film was set during the reign of William III and Mary II (jointly reigned 1698–1694, which served to influence the setting of The League of Gentlemen's feature film (The League of Gentlemen's Apocalypse (2005, dir. Steve Bendelack)). On one of the featurettes included in the 2019 Blu-ray release, Haggard describes the film as set in the 16th century, with its background of religious wars and atmosphere redolent of magic and witchcraft. Howard David Ingham states that the Judge's dialogue indicates that the film is set in the last decade of the 17th century, while Tanya Krzywinska (2017) places it in the early 17th century.

While a date is never explicitly given, the Judge raises a toast to His Catholic Majesty James III, which was the Jacobite title for James Francis Edward Stuart, the Old Pretender (1688–1766). Given that his father, King James II (VII) was deposed in 1688 and died in 1701, the film is most likely set in the first half of the 18th century, either during the reign of Queen Anne (1702-1714) or George I (1714-1727).

THE INFLUENCE OF INGMAR BERGMAN

Haggard (2016) has noted that his style and approach were heavily influenced by Swedish director Ingmar Bergman, particularly his films *The Seventh Seal* (1957) and *The Virgin Spring* (1960). Their approach to sex and death appealed to Haggard, and we can see similarities in style and set pieces in *Satan's Claw*. These Bergman films are grounded in a depiction of a believable and authentic historical rurality where the hard work and daily grind of life for rural communities is not hidden but brought to the fore. The time taken to tend livestock, cook or travel to church, and the details of these activities are dwelt upon. There are also similarities in directorial style. *The Blood on Satan's Claw* opens with a series of shots reminiscent to those in *The Seventh Seal* and *The Virgin Spring*, using low camera angles, framing shots through undergrowth, and presenting characters on high landscapes against the sky. Bergman and Haggard adopt a painterly style, with compositions reminiscent of landscape art. The effect is to cast the characters as diminished agents within a vast and indifferent landscape, and to depersonalise them as little more than silhouettes. Human agency is radically reduced and weakened. There are also similarities in subject matter. Haggard and Bergman are interested in the uncomfortable juxtaposition of rural beauty and rural savagery, with violent acts committed amid scenes of picturesque serenity. Both directors are also fascinated by the mankind's relationship to the spiritual sublime, whether that is a Christian or pagan spirituality. Both Bergman's films and *Satan's Claw* have an unsentimentalised rawness to them and a sense of the closeness of harm and threat in pre-Modern societies.

FOOTNOTES

1. Heyworth would move into television, producing game and reality shows including *Treasure Hunt* (1982-1989; 2002-03), *Challenge Anneka* (1987-1992), and *The Crystal Maze* (1990-1994), while Andrews would go on to direct most episodes of the US soap opera *How to survive a marriage* (1974-75).

2. Gold Winner for Best Drama Special at the 2018 New York Festivals® International Radio Awards

A GREEN AND (UN)PLEASANT LAND

The austere, painterly beauty of the rural landscape © Tigon

The film opens with a shot of Ralph Gower ploughing. The camera is positioned low with Ralph, his horse and plough moving across the horizon in the background. Positioned in the foreground are his victuals, a simple ploughman's lunch. As Ralph moves across the frame the next shot cuts to a close-up of the plough turning the earth, and we hear the sound of the metal cutting and lifting the soil and its wheels grinding across the earth. Throughout these shots the camera maintains a position low to the ground.

Ralph is briefly interrupted in his work by a friendly call from Cathy Vespers, who shouts a greeting from across the field before going on her way, her call to Ralph accompanied on the soundtrack by bird song. During Cathy's interruption, the camera has moved upwards to eye level. After she leaves, Ralph takes a pause in his labours, and in doing so notices a flock of birds converging on a freshly ploughed area of the field. The sound of birds' cawing is quickly accompanied by the first incidental music in the film, an ominous, quavering, high-pitched, pulsing sound, which is then joined by a repeated set of five declining notes, as Ralph heads to see what has attracted the birds' attention.

The camera returns to a position low to the ground as Ralph approaches. He leans over the spot, the camera looking up into Ralph's face, as he squats down. The camera then cuts between two perspectives – that of Ralph looking down at the earth, and from the earth looking up at Ralph – as he moves what looks like a bone out of the way to reveal a fiendish face leering up from the ground. As the music reaches a crescendo there is a crash zoom as the camera dives towards the skull's worm-infested eye, before cutting to a close-up of Ralph's disgusted reaction before he flees across the field. The credits start to roll.

THE RURAL LANDSCAPE

This pre-credits sequence was the first shoot of the film, one that took several hours to complete. It absolutely sums up Haggard's feeling towards the countryside:

> the atmosphere, the depth, the darkness, the distance, the silence, the peace, the furrow, and the camera in the furrow [signifying] what's coming up from down below … [The opening] has the land, it has agricultural labour, young love, the beautiful valley, the earth, the fruitful earth, and who knows what the hell coming up from underneath. (Haggard, 2019)

Fundamental to this scene is the presentation of the countryside as a worked landscape. This is entirely consistent with Haggard's stated intentions for representing the countryside authentically, as an inhabited environment. He was keen to avoid what he described as the theatrical, camp and clichéd horror of Hammer. Hammer's films, he felt were very much a 'product' – entertaining but lacking substance (Haggard, 2016). Haggard had grown up on a farm in Scotland and was familiar with working a tractor and seeing horse-drawn ploughs. His countryside is as a place of hard work and gruelling labour, and not simply a pretty, bucolic backdrop: It is a 'world we are living in' rather than 'a scene we are looking at' (Wylie, 2007: 1). Agricultural work in *Satan's Claw* is presented as an all-encompassing way of life, at the centre of the lives of individuals and the wellbeing of the whole community. His upbringing also emphasised 'the power of the darkness of the countryside' (Haggard, 2019): the back-breaking work, the often pragmatic brutality, the need to work in order to provide essentials like food. While there is a stark grind to working the land, Haggard brings out the intrinsic beauty of this physicality and closeness to the earth. The authenticity of the film certainly caught the imagination of Jeremy Dyson, a member of The League of Gentlemen, who felt that (like *Witchfinder General*) the period is rendered with such believable conviction that it entirely transports you from modern times; there is no sense that you are watching a recreation of Early Modern England or that, at any moment, some element of the modern world might accidentally appear in shot. Instead it feels like a window into an older and tougher time (Haggard, 2019; Dyson on audio commentary).

The faithful rendering of the rural landscape goes beyond the location filming and extends to interiors and studio scenes. Unlike the Baroque lighting of much of Hammer's oeuvre, the filming of *Satan's Claw* attempts to simulate natural light as far as possible and to reflect the general darkness of the period in an age before mass-produced forms of artificial light. The sets are also dressed with great sensitivity to the period, to the location of the film and the social classes of the characters. The proliferation of ornate candelabra often seen in period horror films is conspicuous by its absence here. Instead there are a large number of tapers, demonstrating a greater faithfulness to the 17th and early 18th centuries in the English countryside, as candles were expensive, and most homes were lit by rush-lights and tapers dipped in animal fat. The art department took their research seriously to ensure a faithful match-up of texture and tone between the interior and exterior locations. Similarly faithful in terms of period detail is the carriage that the Judge takes from London back to the village, which is not fitted with glass windows and instead with leather shutters; a far more likely scenario given how expensive glass was (Haggard, 2019; Gatiss on audio commentary). Similarly, Mark is buried in a shroud rather than a coffin, as a coffin would have been prohibitively expensive for rural folk like the Vespers' family. The interiors of the Banham house and the Vespers' cottage also demonstrate the same period fidelity. Rather than being filled with sumptuary and ornamentation the sets are instead muted and bare. Art Director Arnold Chapkis and Set Dresser Milly Burns were heavily influenced by the work of Dutch Golden Age artist Vermeer (1632-1675) in terms of the muted colour palette and plain simplicity of furnishings. As with Vermeer's work, there is an attention to a handful of specific, domestic and generally unremarkable objects (a taper in its holder, a deck of cards, a birdcage) (Haggard, 2019, interview with Burns). Even the lighting and the composition of some of the interior scenes illustrate the influence of Vermeer with an emphasis on the rural simplicity and plainness of daily life. As with the location filming, there is a consistent emphasis on the commonplace, the unaffected and the earthy.

Simple interiors – the influence of Vermeer © Tigon

The opening sequence is characterised by shooting low to the ground with the camera, and by extension the viewer, placed within the furrows of the earth, observing in close detail the action of the plough lifting and turning the soil. Paul Newland has described this attention to the substance of the earth as the 'haptic materiality' of the soil (Newland, 2016: 167), and it is a useful term in conveying the loaminess of the film. Howard David Ingham picks up on this physicality, identifying the connection between the earthiness of the landscape and the earthiness of the cult's activities later on, stating 'It's a grim film. It has dirt caked under its nails' (Ingham, 2018: 26). The camera shots give the earth itself a point of view: it looks up at Ralph, surrounds him and covers him. In doing so, Adam Scovell suggests that the direction gives 'the landscape a palpable, clawing sentience and agency' (Scovell, 2017: 19). There is little in the way of a sentimentalised approach. Beautifully composed though the first shot is – that of Ralph ploughing in the distance – it acts to foreground his victuals, a subtle reminder of the simplicity and frugality of the lives of those who worked the land. The colour palette that Haggard and Director of Photography Dick Bush use is one 'of muted greens and umbers, mud, filth, grey skies and rain' (Young, 2010: 17). There is nothing idealised or bucolic in these colour choices. The palette instead represents the rural landscape using the muddy and wet colours of the English countryside. As with the landscape, the clothes, objects and homes featured in *Satan's Claw* are also rendered in a dull, matt colour palette. Given that rich, deep colours would have necessitated expensive dyes, this is an entirely believable colour palette for a subsistent, rural community. Only the Judge, a wealthier man from a higher social station who hails from London rather than the village, has clothes that feature colours outside of white, black or muted tones. Colours are not the only area of design that are muted: there is very little variety in terms of patterning and textures, and little in the way of ornamentation and flourish. The clothing and materials shown are very much in keeping with a community built around physical, rural labour – rough, unkempt, dirty. Compare this to Hammer's contemporary horror films, *Countess Dracula* (1971, dir. Peter Sasdy) and *Vampire Circus* (1971, dir. Robert Young) for example, which demonstrate a much greater range and richness of texture, colour and pattern, and feature heavily ornamented sets dressed with stained glass, ornate furniture, books, candelabra, cushions, blankets, and other paraphernalia. The Hammer examples also set far more of the action indoors, a marked contrast to *The Blood on Satan's Claw* that situates the bulk of its action outside – in fields, forests, gardens, graveyards and ruins. Even the exterior sequences for *Countess Dracula*, such as the courtyard scenes, were filmed in the studio. The consequence of these differences in design and production is that *Countess Dracula*, like many other examples of Hammer's horror output, places a great emphasis on artificiality and sumptuousness (indeed, one of the defining images from those very first of Hammer's gothic horrors – the gunshot eye of the Monster in *The Curse of Frankenstein* (1957, dir. Terence Fisher) and the gore splashed over the tomb in the opening credits for *Dracula* (1958, dir. Terence Fisher) – was the copious use of bright scarlet theatrical blood), while *The Blood on Satan's Claw* instead stresses authenticity and austerity. This is entirely in keeping with Haggard's stated desire to avoid the excesses of Hammer's gothic horror films.

THE PASTORAL LANDSCAPE

This is not to say that Haggard ignores the beauty of the rural landscape in favour of the physicality of the worked countryside: rather he finds that there is a beauty in rural labour. Even the first shot, with the camera at the level of the earth observing the distant Ralph, frames the mise-en-scène in the manner of a 19th-century landscape scene, a 'distinctly painterly view' of the countryside (Newland, 2016: 166), with Ralph moving almost in a two-dimensional fashion from right to left across the horizon against the background of the sky. The business of farming is set alongside the austere beauty of the field.

Ralph is interrupted in his work by a friendly call from Cathy, across the field on the edge of the woods. The camera assumes a position from behind Cathy, nestled in the trees. Her greeting is accompanied by sweet birdsong, and she faces a beautiful blue sky. There is a pastoral pleasance to the scene, a sense of serenity and events passing as expected and desired. In common with the opening shot of Ralph ploughing against the horizon, the framing shot of Cathy against the forest edge has a sense of the Victorian landscape tradition to it. There is a contentment and constancy to the scene, not only because of the geniality between Cathy and Ralph but also because of their evident comfort and familiarity with their environment. This is a content community, fully cognisant of their daily and seasonal activities. The peacefulness of the countryside – the clear weather, the birdsong, the bucolic rolling hills – all suggest a rural idyll in which time and life are passing in harmony and as expected and desired.

The watchful countryside – peering out from behind the undergrowth © Tigon

In some ways this sense of peace and constancy, if not the haptic physicality of the soil, is very similar to the depiction of the rural landscape in heritage drama, a term that has become used to describe a range of screen texts that commoditise the English rural and historical landscape into a marketable and commercial form. The heritage drama landscape is overwhelmingly rural and pastoral, and frequently used in conjunction with a narrative set in the past, associating a heritage landscape to heritage culture. Examples are varied as the heritage film can be found across a wide range of genres and styles, but include celebrated British 'art-house' films such as *Chariots of Fire* (1981, dir. Hugh Hudson), *A Room with a View* (1985, dir. James Ivory), and *Howards End* (1992, dir. James Ivory); historical dramas like *Elizabeth* (1998, dir. Shekhar Kapur) and *Mrs Brown* (1997, dir. John Madden), and television series from *Brideshead Revisited* (1981) to *Downton Abbey* (2010-2015, 2019). Peter Hutchings notes the criticism aimed at heritage drama and film 'associated as they are with a prettified, escapist marketing of an unreal image of Britain and British life' (Hutchings, 2004: 28).

THE UNCANNY LANDSCAPE

The countryside of *Satan's Claw* is more complex than this though. The gently rolling hills, the broad fields, and the open, blue sky may be beautiful but they also emphasise the considerable scale of the rural landscape. In *Satan's Claw*, the sharp cut between the close-ups of Ralph working the land and the long shot of Cathy calling to him across the fields reduces them to small and solitary figures within the vast landscape. Those two establishing shots, from Ralph's point of view and then from Cathy's, illustrate the enormity of the landscape, the breadth and number of the fields, the distance from the rest of the village, and the complete absence (aside from themselves) of any other human habitation. While they are close enough to call to each other, they are nonetheless a considerable distance apart. The effect of this distancing and reducing is, in the words of Derek Johnston, 'a shift in perception from the idyllic to the ominous' (Johnston, 2017). The scale of the rural vista in the opening sequence of *Satan's Claw* highlights how remote the characters are from each other, and how far the community is from any other settlements. The reduction in the scale of Ralph and Cathy also reduces down their lives and activities; it is 'a sudden awareness of human insignificance in relation to the natural world' (ibid.). Despite the sound of the birds there is an inanimacy to the countryside; there is no movement beyond Ralph and Cathy's activities. The overall effect is to disconnect the characters not only from each other, and their community for any other community, but also from the rural landscape that surrounds them. It is interesting that, despite much of the action taking place in exteriors filmed on location (and therefore authentically outside), the film has an enclosing, claustrophobic feeling. Isolated as it is within a rural landscape that it is disconnected from, the village becomes a hermetic space.

The film's score is critical in building this sense of unease. It tells us that the countryside, while apparently serene, is not to be trusted. The move away from traditional orchestral sound and the use of period instrumentation gives the score an otherworldly quality and marks it out as unusual for contemporaneous films, providing a distinctive fluidity that 'lulls you then it twists and squeezes and squirms' (Wynne-Simmons, 2019). In composing the score, Marc Wilkinson researched witchcraft in 17th-century England and America, as well as the styles of music of the period. As such, the score feels historical (here are notable similarities to melodies like *Greensleeves* and other folk pastoral music), and natural (influenced as it is by the sense of birdsong and the wind) but dissonant and unsettling, due in part to the composition featuring a chromatic scale starting with a high B that omitted the augmented 5th (known, aptly enough, as the Devil's Interval) (Haggard, 2019, interview with Wilkinson).

The credits continue the disquieting ambiguity of the landscape. Initial close-ups of crows against an overcast sky give way to stark images of bare twigs in extreme close-up. Despite the grim beauty of these natural elements, it suggests an inhospitable and unforgiving landscape, barren rather than bountiful and unfriendly to human habitation. As Scovell notes, 'the evil is given an avarian symbolism over a landscape montage' (Scovell, 2017: 20) and this is a symbolism that continues throughout the course of the film. The crow of course has long been associated in European and British folklore with misfortune, death and the afterlife. The rural landscape then, despite its beauty and serenity, is one with uneasy undercurrents of threat and menace. It is an environment with the potential both for sustenance and nurture, but also for alienation and harm.

These curious and apparently contradictory juxtapositions characterise the countryside of *The Blood on Satan's Claw* as an uncanny landscape. The uncanny is a concept that Sigmund Freud developed in his eponymous essay of 1919, and is an approximate translation of his term 'unheimliche' that more accurately translates as 'unhomely'. Freud relates the uncanny to what is frightening, but determines that the uncanny describes a specific trope that exists within the spectrum of causes of dread and horror. For Freud the uncanny is 'that species of the frightening that goes back to what was once well known and had long been familiar' (Freud translated by McLintock, 2003: 124). He more broadly associates this with uncertainty, in particular an uncertainty over familiarity. He begins his consideration of the uncanny by ruminating on the uncertainty created by human-like objects, such as dolls, waxworks and automata, postulating on E Jentsch's assertion that these items are uncanny to us as they leave us uncertain as to whether 'an apparently animate object is really alive and, conversely, whether a lifeless object might not perhaps be animate' (Jentsch quoted by Freud, translated by McLintock, 2003: 135). The uncertainty, and thus the uncanniness, arises from our doubts over whether something that appears long familiar to us, like the human form, is actually instead unfamiliar (in these examples by virtue of being facsimiles of human life). Freud goes on to suggest that this uncertainty over familiarity is linked to repetition: the recurrence of familiarity until, through the acts of recurrence, the familiar becomes unfamiliar.

Following this definition, the countryside of *Satan's Claw* is an uncanny landscape. It reaches back to those notions of the rural landscape that we long cherish as familiar, often from childhood. The association with holidays and picnics, with fruitfulness and provision, with nature, health and vitality, all culturally embed the countryside within the collective unconscious as a locus for a nostalgic and happy familiarity. The film opens with Ralph ploughing the field, an activity he is entirely familiar with, one we can reasonably imagine he has been doing almost his whole life, and one that he would have seen his father perform, going back generations. His and Cathy's friendly greeting to each other, accompanied by birdsong and set amongst the rolling meadows, speaks to us of a community that feels safe, settled and secure. To use Freud's terms, this is a landscape that is well known and long familiar. Our introduction to this rurality via Ralph and Cathy, both adolescents, implicitly associates the countryside with youth, and appeals to the viewer's nostalgia for the countryside and plays on their feelings of familiarity too.

However, our certainty in this familiar scene is confounded by objects and activities that we do not associate with the countryside. The discovery of repulsive items, such as the demonic remains and the patches of fur that grow on the bodies of the village youths, the use of long abandoned sites like the ruins in the forest and the attic of the Banham house, and the interruption made by brutal activities, all sow doubts in our minds, and those of the characters, as to how familiar this rural landscape actually is. The origination of the remains from the field suggest they are a product of the rural landscape and one we can infer predates human settlement. Its subsequent occupation of those spaces long abandoned for human use, and its inspiration of acts of savagery within the community, challenges the notion of the familiar countryside. The uncanny landscape catalyses the degradation of the previously tranquil community, not only through violent acts, but also in the breakdown of familial and neighbourly bonds as parental figures turn against children and the village Curate is accused of abuse.

THE MALIGN LANDSCAPE

Beyond a form of inanimate, uncanny disquiet, the countryside in *The Blood on Satan's Claw* could also be considered to be an actively malignant agent. Despite its apparent beauty and tranquillity, the rural landscape nurtures and conceals the malevolence that threatens the village. It is from the earth that the demonic remains emerge; while Ralph's plough unwittingly turns the diabolic remnants up, his ignorance of their existence prior to their unearthing, and their location so close to the soil surface suggest that the countryside has almost a sentient capacity in either permitting or encouraging the emergence and discovery of the remains. The low angle of the earth in the opening sequence 'instantly places a malevolence upon its soil … as if the earth is glaring at him [Ralph]' (Scovell, 2017: 19), the camera work bestowing a spiteful agency upon the land. Later, when the cult brings Cathy before the fiend, Margaret reads aloud from the Book of the Beast reciting 'Rise now from the forests, from the furrows, from the fields and live', explicitly identifying the devil with the rural landscape like some ancient god of the wilderness. The apparently friendly greeting that Cathy gives to Ralph during the pre-credits sequence is also open to more complex interpretations. Cathy is not facing the camera; instead it sits behind her, observing her through the trees. This puts the viewer in a voyeuristic position, secretly watching Cathy as she goes about her business. The anonymous peering out from between the trees assumes the position of a hidden, sylvan agency, like a woodland beast or dryadic creature, on the part of the viewer. As such, we are unsure of our agency as the viewer in observing the scene, leaving it ambiguous whether Cathy is alone (aside from Ralph) or whether she is in danger. Bush was instrumental in these shots of characters seen through occlusive foliage, usually putting the viewer in the wooded or dense undergrowth and peering out at characters going about their business in more open surroundings like fields and clearings. The consequence of this artful cinematography is the near constant suggestion that our characters are under the watchful gaze of clandestine entities from the wilderness, or from the wilderness itself. The characters' lack of awareness that they are under observation, and the apparent boldness of the secret observer, adds a frisson of menace. Robert Macfarlane (2015) identifies a similar sense of uneasy observation in MR James' *A View From A Hill*, in which protagonist Fanshawe feels he is being observed from within the woods with malign interest. The countryside then, far from being a placid environment, is instead actively malign in observing the villagers and causing them harm.

THE RESISTANT LANDSCAPE

The landscape, as the context from which the fiend emerges, and as a watchful and malign presence observing the characters, is in apparent conflict with the village that it has sustained for generations. The presence of the Judge, as an interloper from nearby London, could be considered a catalyst. *The Blood on Satan's Claw* is by no means unusual for its time in exploring the contentious relationship between the modern, homogenising and outwardly encroaching urban centre and the rural periphery, which is at risk of disappearing in the face of this incursion. The 1960s and 1970s saw a number of British films and television programmes address this time and again. Frequently the centre was associated with a reduction in individual and time-honoured liberties, state direction and its efforts to control greater and more aspects of everyday life: for example, *The Prisoner* (1967) is entirely based around the efforts of the individual to resist assimilation into the bureaucratised, state driven collective. There were also films and programmes that explored the need for the centre to maintain order and exert control over highly stylised and individualised threats from the periphery, such as *The Avengers* (1961-1969), *The New Avengers* (1976-1977) and, in an even more abstract fashion, *Sapphire and Steel* (1979-1982). The anxiety caused by the disappearance of rural communities and distinctive ways of life in the face of a homogeneous and encroaching centre is articulated through television plays like *Penda's Fen* (1974, dir. Alan Clarke) and *Requiem for a Village* (1976, dir. David Gladwell), while even a comedy like *The Good Life* (1975-1978) depicts the conflict that arises when the homogenous 'civilised' culture is interrupted by 'an anarchic, atavistic spark that re-invokes a rhythm that has been lost under urban tarmac and clock (on) time' (Krzywinska, 2017). More recently, the comedy *Detectorists* (BBC, 2014-2017) also explores this tension between rural antiquity and urban modernity, and shares similar (if far less horrifying) concerns to *The Blood on Satan's Claw*: that the earth and the rural landscape are not subordinate to us but must be treated with respect and not a little awe; that the earth is a material that must be worked (whether by plough or by metal detector) and that working the land forms the backbone of everyday life; that the earth has dirty, physical dimensions and depths as soil to be dug and trudged through; and that the earth has secrets and hidden spaces through which the past can manifest.

Even more so than *Detectorists*, perhaps the best contemporary expression of the tension between the expanding, homogenising centre and the resistant, distinctive periphery is another recent comedy, *The League of Gentlemen* (1997, 1999-2002, 2005, 2017). The key storyline that explores this tension is that of the local shop and the new road. The local shop is run by Tubbs and Edward (played by Steve Pemberton and Reece Shearsmith respectively), an odd couple who are revealed to be brother and sister engaged in an incestuous relationship and who (especially Edward) aggressively resist the encroachment of anything or anyone unfamiliar to them with the famous cry of 'we are a local shop for local people, there's nothing for you here!'. Over the course of the first series they become aware that a new road is being built to allow for improved access into the town, and that it will necessitate the demolition of their shop. The danger then to Tubbs and Edward is twofold: firstly, the threat of an influx of strangers to their shop, and secondly, the threat of the destruction of their home. The parochialism of Tubbs and Edward is a peculiar one; their supposedly local shop is located far from the centre of Royston Vasey, apparently in the middle of nowhere, occupying a liminal threshold between the town and the wider world, and peripheral to both. As such their insistence that they are 'a local shop' is an odd one, as it does not appear to serve any community. Arguably the only community the shops services is that of Tubbs and Edward themselves. It is a hermetic community of two, and one that is so insulated, even from the nearby Royston Vasey, as to have its own economy (based on the totemic, rather than monetary, value of the stock, as they have no desire to sell any of the 'precious things of the shop') and language (a corrupted, regressed and almost childlike form of English) (Hunt, 2008: 64). In some ways they are analogous to the Banham house in *Satan's Claw*, a place of local significance (as the local manor) that sits at the periphery of the village. Also, like the local shop and its associated threat from the new road, the Banham house is the first threatened with destruction by the diabolical remains as it apparently drives Rosalind Barton mad and causes her physical transformation, catalyses the disappearance of Isobel Banham, and leads Peter Edmonton to mutilate himself. The difference here though is that the Banham house is threatened with destruction from the emergent force within the village and not from outside it like the shop in *The League of Gentlemen*. A closer analogy would be to compare Tubbs and Edward themselves to the diabolical remains. Like the remains, Tubbs and Edward are represented as a dormant force violently awakened by an intrusive presence. The local shop is dark, dusty and cobwebbed, like a slumbering tomb. They are awakened by the unwitting interruption caused by outsiders entering the shop for directions or to browse. In disturbing the slumber of Tubbs and Edward they unknowingly cause their own doom.

The very notion of 'local' in *Satan's Claw* – coded explicitly as rural, primitive and uncivilised – is a fundamental threat to urban culture and society. Similarly the 'local' of *The League of Gentlemen* presents us with characters who are 'local' in the same sense of being anathema to our urban civilisation – Tubbs and Edward are not only an incestuous couple, but one who are strongly implied to indulge in bestiality and also to commit murder; the toad-obsessed Dentons form a closed family that is utterly alien to their nephew (an interloper from the urban centre) Benjamin, and one whose views are so extreme as to offend civilised values; the butcher Hilary Briss is heavily implied to be serving human flesh to his customers. Even the sequences featuring well-meaning vet Mr Chinnery, that reference the more idealised, nostalgic rural landscapes of programmes like *All Creatures Great and Small* (1978-1990), end with the unpleasant demise of pets and thus send up the notion of the rose-tinted, bucolic countryside (Hunt, 2008: 67). 'Local' then, in both *The League of Gentlemen* and *Satan's Claw*, is synonymous with thoroughly uncivilised values and savage behaviours.

NATURE AND CIVILISATION

The village in *The Blood on Satan's Claw* is a community isolated by, and within, the vast panorama of the English countryside. The only other settlement mentioned is London, which is where the Judge goes to halfway through the film. The village is bordered by spaces both cultivated (the fields) and uncultivated (the forest).

The character of these three environments – London, the village and its cultivated environs, and the uncultivated wilderness – and the relationship between them, is of critical importance to the narrative of *Satan's Claw*. This chapter will explore these characteristics and the nature of the antagonistic relationships between them.

LONDON

London is the only settlement outside the village to be seen and mentioned, and even then, only once. About 30 minutes into the film, and following Peter Edmonton's frenzied self-mutilation, the Judge makes the decision to head there with the Doctor's book on magical beliefs to attend to matters of business. We then see London – or at least the interior of the Judge's house in London – at an hour in, when Peter Edmonton rides to tell him of the brutality that has overtaken the village. The Judge advises Peter that there is more than witchcraft at work, and that he is ready to return.

London, then, is used to demark sections of the narrative: the first third of the film, up to the point when the Judge leaving for the capital, sees the demonic force influence unearthed and then exert its evil influence in the Banham household; the middle part of the film, between the Judge leaving and then returning, sees the evil force move into the wilderness and draw a coven under the leadership of Angel Blake; the final third, after the Judge returns, sees the villagers fight back against the coven. It is perhaps understandable, given the initial plans for a portmanteau structure, that the plot functions in this triptych fashion with the journeys to and from London effectively closing chapters of the narrative. Beyond this though, London is used to represent a civilising and progressive force that opposes the regressive and rural force of the demon.

The late 17th and 18th centuries saw a number of gradual, but no less profound, changes to the traditional society, economy and culture of Britain. The Scientific Revolution and the Enlightenment both proposed a rational, reasoned examination of the natural world, one that celebrated man's ability to question and understand rather than merely ascribe everything to divine agency. This optimistic attention to man's capacity to comprehend the world around him through reason and rationality was summed up by the phrase 'Sapere aude' (dare to know), taken from the Roman poet Horace by Immanuel Kant for his essay 'Answering the question: What is the Enlightenment?' (1784). By the late 18th century, Britain had marched inexorably towards becoming an industrialised, urbanised and mechanised society, with the construction of canals starting from the 1740s and industrial towns growing rapidly (Birmingham, for example, saw its population almost double between 1731 and 1778 from 23,286 to 42,250) (Anon, 'Historical population of Birmingham'; Anon, 'Birmingham MB/CB historical statistics'; Anon, 'Birmingham office for national statistics'). These were, of course, slow and incremental changes. In 1900, one in ten workers was still engaged in agricultural work, and agriculture remained the single biggest employer until the 1901 census. Also, while farming was increasingly influenced by mechanisation from the mid-18th century onwards, it was haphazard and piecemeal; for example, while threshing machines were introduced from the 1760s, ploughing using horses, as we see Ralph doing at the start of the film, continued virtually unchanged until the end of the 19th century as the mechanical alternatives were, in the most part, prohibitively expensive (Payne, 1994; 6, 21).

Graduality of changes notwithstanding, some communities would have started to experience the effects of creeping urbanisation and mechanisation sooner than others. Additionally, looking back over the centuries and with the benefit of hindsight, we distinguish patterns of inexorable change – a movement from rural to urban, from manual to mechanical, from agriculture to industry – and perceive moments and environments on the cusp of experiencing them. This appreciation of hindsight is especially influential on film makers who will capture the breadth of the impact of these slow, generational changes in a single film. The village in *Satan's Claw* is exactly that, featuring a community that, from our modern perspective, will gradually experience these progressive and profound changes.

The scene set in what we can reasonably infer is the London home of the Judge may be brief but it is instructive in how it differs from our exploration of the village. As previously discussed, we only experience London through this small studio set, rather than the expansive location filming for the village. In the Judge's home we see evidence of learning: the many bookshelves in the background and the quill pens in the foreground both attest to this. In contrast, we only ever see two books in the village: the tome of the Doctor's on magical and supernatural beliefs, and the mysterious book of Behemoth that Margaret reads from before Cathy's rape and murder. The Judge is dressed in a sumptuous, fur-lined robe, a marked contrast to the simple, tonally muted garb of the countryfolk in the village. The Judge also wears glasses in this scene for the only time in the film; this attests to his education (as he is wearing them in his study it is safe to assume they are reading glasses) and his wealth (as they were luxury items). The study is also clean and precise, a marked difference from the earthiness of the village countryside. Through this short, studio-based scene, London is presented as affluent and educated, but also perhaps artificial and ephemeral, a stark contrast to the long shots of the rural landscape that establish the village as something rooted, permanent and real. Represented through this scene of sumptuary, learning and meticulousness, London is defined as a seat of wealth, knowledge and reason – a hub of modernity. The obeisance that the other characters, especially the Squire, make to the Judge is not just respectful of the Judge's social position but also, by extension, the Judge's urban environment. Thus, the city is placed in a superior position to the countryside. With the elevation of the city comes the elevation of all that the city represents: modernity, reason, progress. Conversely, with the subordination of the rural landscape, comes the subordination of those values associated with it: heritage, tradition, constancy.

THE WILDERNESS

The uncultivated wilderness is one that sees the least activity in terms of being adapted for human habitation, use and consumption. Often these are wild meadows, forests, seaways, uninhabited distant islands, caves, and mountains, either difficult to access or challenging to be utilised to support human civilisation. Not only, then, are these locales virtually untouched by human activity – such as settlement building, logging, fishing or farming – but they have often not even been mapped and charted thoroughly.

While attractive in their lack of occupation and spoliation through human activity, it is paradoxically this same absence of human presence that makes these spaces so disquieting. The tension between these apparently binary characteristics marks these wild spaces out as uncanny landscapes: sites both of awe and beauty because of their unspoilt nature and unmapped terrain, but also threat and apprehension because of the vacancy of civilisation.

In *Satan's Claw*, the uncultivated wilderness is the woodland beyond the village that houses the ruins, that provides the space in which the fiend and its cult make their home and carry out their brutal rituals. While the youth of the community – Ralph, Cathy and Mark – are very familiar with the topography of the village and its cultivated spaces, the woods represent something far more complex. It is a space that is free from the strict demarcations of the village, and as such is a space they play in and roam through freely. In contrast to the village, in which space is controlled and allocated specific function within a socio-economic hierarchy through fences, pens and hedges, the absence of the influence of civilisation in the woodland is consequentially the absence of imposed socio-economic control over the land. The cult is therefore free to use the woodland as it wishes and impose its own forms of control and demarcation. For example, the ruins are established by the cult to be the sacred hub of authority within the wilderness, to which spot sacrificial victims are drawn and where the demon makes its home. However, because it is an uncharted space, it is separated from any protection and surveillance the village may offer. The only sign of human occupation within the forest are the ruins, the site of the cult's rituals. The ruins appear to be a former church (unsurprising given that the location used are the ruins of St James' Old Church in Bix) but there is no explicit diegetic acknowledgement that this is so. The ruins symbolise the retreat of human occupation from the woods. They suggest that at one point there was some form of permanent settlement there, or at least an established sacred space within the wilderness. Consequently, the film makes a direct association between the wilderness and an absence of civilisation and civilised values.

There was no distinction within pre-agricultural societies between the wilderness and other environments. The development of cultivation and the domestication of animals led to the subsequent categorisation of land into the cultivated and that which had not been cultivated yet. Until the 18th century, the uncultivated wilderness was feared, a

The sacred wilderness © Tigon

place alive with spirits. Forests and mountains in particular were considered to be the home of evil spirits in the Mediaeval and Early Modern periods. Not only was the wilderness frightening because it was a place beyond human reach, it was frightening because of the influence it could have on drawing people away from civilisation; it was considered to have a dangerous influence on 'uncivilising' people. Those who spent too long in the wilderness ran the risk of becoming part of it; isolated within these large and remote landscapes, individuals could regress to savage, uncivilised behaviours (Short, 1991: 9). Civilisation is presented as something that is only skin deep, and the wilderness quickly deteriorates it until the savagery present beneath emerges. Newland makes a connection between the activities of the characters within the cultivated space – farming and agricultural work that is required to maintain order and control over the landscape – and the behaviour of the youthful cult members in the woodlands, who appear to spy and peer between the branches and play amongst the trees in the manner of sprites, nymphs and satyrs (Newland, 2016: 168).

Our perceptions of the wilderness have been shaped by Classical and Romantic attitudes. The Classical attitude to the wilderness considers that 'human use confers meaning on space' (Short, 1991: 6). A characteristic of civilisation is the transformation of physical space for human habitation and cultivation. Human civilisation and society give meaning and sense to the landscape, and those areas that sit beyond the space that has been defined by civilisation are to be feared. This attitude perceives a linear, progressive model of time – a trajectory of improvement, modernity and progress. The counter attitude was the Romantic one in which the wilderness has 'a purity which human contact tends to sully and degrade' (ibid.). The space untouched by civilisation is to be celebrated and revered as awesome, as it represents a historic past that is a state of grace, closer to nature, from which we have fallen and continue to fall. The Romantic perception has gained traction in the Modern period, as the wilderness has been transformed over time from a vast and encroaching landscape to an environment under threat from human encroachment. Rather than representing a fearful absence of civilised authority, the Romantic attitude celebrates the wilderness because of this absence of civilised authority; there is a virtue and natural truth there that has been lost in the artifice and falsity of civilisation. A return to nature was felt to offer spiritual regeneration and self-knowledge, and arguably this is something that the fiend offers to the cult, albeit one of a malign and destructive kind.

The Classical notion of cultivating the wilderness is one that sat at the very centre of Mediaeval and Early Modern thought. The Bible (and ergo all history according to contemporary philosophies) began with the divine creation of the Garden of Eden; as such, cultivation of the wilderness was divinely directed – the subduing and control of wilderness and fashioning according to a design. This functioned as a rationale for cutting forests, draining fens, reclaiming heaths, for cultivatable land. *The Blood on Satan's Claw* mediates this tension between the encroachment of civilisation and the aggressive response by the wilderness.

The Romantic attitude is a harking back to the traditions of nature worship in antiquity, particularly with regard to Roman beliefs, which considered the physical landscape to be occupied by genii locorum, guardian spirits that were worshipped and venerated for the protection they offered. The majority were associated with natural features: mountains, trees, forests, meadows, springs, rivers, caves and lakes. The veneration of these spirits saw, by extension, the veneration of the place protected by the spirit; as such, these natural features become both sites of reverence and sites to be revered. These spirits could take the form of nymphs, fauns and satyrs, and the physiognomy and folklore associated with them demonstrates the active relationship between the spirit and the wilderness: fauns and satyrs, as beings that are half human and half goat, are a physical fusion of the human and natural worlds; nymphs, frequently associated with myths that see them transformed into trees, springs and flowers, similarly demonstrate a malleability between civilisation and nature (Legard, 2015: 366-367). *Satan's Claw*, with its ruined site of worship located within the dense forest, demonstrates this numinous sense of natural veneration. The film presents a wild landscape where, in the words of Gail-Nina Anderson, 'there might be a nymph for every stream, a wild wood full of Dionysiac satyrs and a glade where the goat-footed god could be encountered' (Anderson, 2019: 39). While the city of London might present us with an environment built by man and orientated around mankind's concerns to learn, to progress and to impose order upon the world, the forest is a realm outside of human control and habitation, one in which nature is not subservient and subordinated to man's designs but is instead held in awe as a focus of veneration.

The setting for *The Blood on Satan's Claw* – at some point in the early half of the 18th century – is an appropriate one for exploring the fraught dynamic between the cultivated and uncultivated landscape, sitting as it does on the cusp of the Agrarian and Industrial Revolutions. It also sits at a point where attitudes to landscape, in particular the private landscapes of the estates of the upper classes, were changing. The traditional English garden, one that was formal and symmetrical, had fallen out of taste in favour of landscapes that were designed to appear asymmetrical and informal. Over the course of the 18th century, as the Enlightenment focus on reason and rationality was challenged by the Romantic emphasis on emotion and imagination, the fashion for gardens moved increasingly to the pastoral and representing a perception of the natural landscape as an antique, rural wilderness as a reaction to the imposed and rigid formality of earlier gardens and cultivated spaces. The trappings of the uncultivated wilderness as a site for the veneration of spirits of nature were imported to decorate the estates of the nobility and landed gentry, to ape the sublime beauty of nature. Consequently, many estates were ornamented with Classical statuary, springs, fountains, grottoes, ruins, temples, and monoliths (Short, 1991: 16).

The antique tradition of the wilderness, then, was one in which the rural landscape itself was both the site, and object, of veneration. Conversion to Christianity saw these traditions evolve over time, with some spirits adopted into Mediaeval Christianity as local saints, and many others either demonised or forgotten. Those former pagan sites of worship – the temples, altars and shrines established to the genii locorum

— and those landscapes particularly associated with the veneration of these spirits, fell into disuse following Christianisation. The desacralisation of these spaces and the reorientation of civilisation onto new Christian structures — the Church and its buildings, rituals and hierarchies — led to the abandonment of the previously revered features of the rural landscape. Given that these features were no longer regarded as sacred, the dispossessed genii evolved from protective spirits into supernatural beings that haunted features of the abandoned rural landscape. The forests, springs, caves, heaths and woods cease to be sites of veneration, as worship moves towards the church that is most commonly located as the centre of settlements, rather than at is periphery as had been the case with the shrines dedicated to the spirits of the natural world. This sees a re-orientation of civilisation's outlook in the Mediaeval period onto the Church, located at the urban centre, surrounded by the occupied spaces of towns and cultivated landscapes, with the now abandoned wilderness now at the margins. The wilderness, no longer a sacred space, over time ceases to be familiar and instead becomes associated with mystery and threat, with the former spiritual guardians now perceived as malign, haunting presences. As such, the former sites of pagan worship became regarded as places of danger, as the homes of monsters, or the sites for executions and violent death (Legard, 2015: 368-370). We see this pattern of movement from the sacred periphery to the sacred centre very clearly in *Satan's Claw*, with the former represented by the ruins, and the latter represented by the Reverend Fallowfield's church within the village boundary. The vacated, forsaken sacred space in the woods, once a site for nature to be venerated, instead falls to ruin, reclaimed by nature, and becomes home for the worship of darker, older forces that are inimical to civilisation. It does indeed become a locus of violence, death and brutality. Anderson's mention of 'a wild wood full of Dionysiac satyrs' is an extremely apt phrase that can be applied to the cult in *Satan's Claw*. The youthful cult indulges in behaviour that could easily be described as a Bacchanalian frenzy, in which they cause mutilation and savagery under the sway of an almost mystical and ecstatic insanity. The nakedly lustful gazes of both Angel and Margaret as Cathy is brutalised during the rape scene, and in particular Angel's licking of the shears used to kill Cathy, can only suggest a form of bestial, orgiastic madness of the kind described as associated with Dionysos, Pan, and their retinue of satyrs in Classical mythology. The wilderness then sees an association between the sacred and the bestial.

Those characteristics that identify the wilderness as a sacred and sublime landscape – its remoteness, inaccessibility, human vacancy, and the absence of civilisation – are the same characteristics that also define the space as anathema to human presence. The active hostility to civilisation enables the continuation of behaviours and activities considered contrary to civilisation.

THE VILLAGE

The village represents the point at which the opposing influences of civilisation and nature meet; it is the threshold between the two and where the mutual existence of both can be seen. The rationality of the city can be seen in the management of agriculture, the demarcation of fields for ploughing, of land for livestock, and private spaces for the local gentry. It can also be seen in the social hierarchy, with the local elders – the Doctor, the Curate and the Squire – deferring to the Judge and to the Banham family, their social superiors. The village is a community hub within its locality but is itself peripheral in relation to the much larger hub of the city. As such, and from the perspective of the Judge and the city, the village finds itself existing at the periphery, far closer to the influence of the desacralised wilderness. Despite the organisation of society and land along civilised lines, the influence of the wilderness can be felt too. The Judge notes with scorn how quick the villagers are to look for a supernatural explanation for the diabolical remains. Despite medicine being a profession which we would normally associate with the rational and the modern, the Doctor bases much of his opinion on folkloric beliefs, including a fervent trust in the existence of witchcraft and magic. The Banham household, the social link between the village and the city, finds itself denigrated and destroyed by the influence of the wilderness, the occupants driven to acts of madness and cruelty.

The occupation and demarcation of the village and the Banham farmhouse contrasts with the openness of the fields and the wilderness of the woodland. We first see these aspects at the conclusion of the opening credits, as Ralph runs through the enclosed, private land of the Banham family to the manor house. The Banham farmland, as presented to us from the first time we see it, is defined by its fences, gates and animal pens – a series of obstacles Ralph must navigate to access the house. This 'enclosedness' can be read in terms of the accelerated move towards land enclosure: the practise of seizing smallholdings and consolidating them into larger farms, effectively moving land from common to private ownership. Enclosure was common practice in England from the early 16th century until into the 19th century, although frequently controversial. Enclosure fundamentally changed not only English society, by transferring more direct control over larger tracts of land to a smaller number of affluent landowners, but also the English landscape, by containing and demarking open common land into private smallholdings. As a consequence, farms moved from their traditional location at the centre of villages to the periphery of rural communities, allowing for greater control and expansion on the part of the landowner (Hoskins, 2005: 166). These forms of control and demarcation – straight lines of fences and hawthorn bushes – would become a common sight across the English landscape and are visible in *Blood on Satan's Claw*.

Initial government opposition to enclosure in the 16th and 17th centuries was mediated by an awareness of the commercial advantages of enclosure and the realisation that wholesale depopulation did not necessarily have to accompany it: instead the preference was for enclosure to be agreed mutually by all parties rather than forcibly enforced. Enclosure fundamentally redrew parishes that had looked the same for hundreds of years: new roads, the dividing down of large open fields, the moving of farmsteads outwards from the village centres. It was not only farmland that faced enclosure; there was a large amount of clearing and enclosing woodland too, particularly during the early 17th century as royal forests were sold by James I and Charles I to be cleared for arable farming as well as for farmsteads (Reed, 1997: 206). This clearing could cause local dissent as there were often free grazing rights in the woods for animals. By the early 18th century the drawbacks of enclosure by agreement of all parties were more apparent, as they could be snarled up in legal proceedings, and instead there was a greater move towards acts of parliament for enclosures. Despite this though, there was never any centralised or strategic government push for land enclosure, nor was the open field system ever officially abolished. The process of enclosure led to numerous hawthorn hedgerows, new straight roads with grass verges (Reed, 1997: 242). *The Blood on Satan's Claw*, then, presents us with a community experiencing another gradual yet profound change, that of the change in land ownership from common to private and the consequential changes to the geography and topography of village communities.

Enclosure and enclosedness © Tigon

The English landscape of *Satan's Claw*, then, is one that shows a nascent, if accelerating, imposition of human control over the form and function of the countryside: the enclosed lands of the Banham house defined by fences and pens, the cultivated field ploughed by Ralph into straight furrows. Contemporary opinion considered that cultivated land was far preferable to uncultivated land because it demonstrated order, intelligence and structure (Newland, 2016: 168). It is therefore very suggestive that the film opens with a landscape that demonstrates the beginnings of a systematic 'civilising' of the countryside with Ralph's ploughing of the field into straight furrows, and one that makes clearly apparent the relationship between the management of the earth and the integrity of the social hierarchy that sits above it. As soon as Ralph unearths the diabolical remains he hastens, not to a tavern or to a neighbour's house, but to the landowner's manor, clearly demonstrating how ingrained those social structures are. It is important to stress that this is an emerging and small civilised outpost, rather than a larger and more established rural town. The small scale of the village, coupled with its apparent isolation within the vast rural landscape, and the tentative suggestions of structured and enclosed agriculture, emphasise its potential fragility and its vulnerability in the face of the uncivilising force of the fiendish entity.

THE FIEND AND ITS FOLLOWERS

The village in *Satan's Claw* is a community at the periphery of both civilisation and wilderness, an environment little changed by human activity and therefore closer to a time before civilisation. It is an immemorial landscape, our past given geographic and geologic form. It is unsurprising then that the fiend's skull, a relic from an older, darker past, should manifest so far from modernity:

> coming out of the countryside ... what seems to be beautiful countryside brings forth out of the furrows these dark, dark memories of some earlier religion which wasn't too nice. People don't quite know what they're dealing with at first.
> (Wynne-Simmons, 2019)

What we see in *Satan's Claw* is the deliberate return of a past that refuses to be forgotten, and which, in returning, causes those past traumas to be re-experienced in a present that has forgotten how to overcome them.

ACTS OF OBLIVION

The past, through agency by landscapes like the ruins, objects like the skull, or simple memories, has a 'lasting potency' (Lowenthal, 2015: 136) empowering it to exert an authority on the present. This was appreciated at the time that *Satan's Claw* was set, in the late 17th and early 18th centuries, and because of this the wholesale destruction of the past was required to preserve the present and safeguard the future. The use of oblivion and the obliteration of reminders or memories of the past was thought necessary to ensure the continuity and survival of new creeds, beliefs and behaviours. An example that would have been a historical lesson to those at the time of *Satan's Claw* was the whitewashing of paintings and smashing of images in churches as England moved from Catholicism to Protestantism from the mid-16th century. Much closer to the home period of *Satan's Claw* would have been the Acts of Oblivion in 1660 and 1690. These Acts pardoned those who had opposed Charles II and William III respectively, and are examples of 'remedial oblivion' (Lowenthal, 2015: 139), the collective forgetting of a past trauma to enable a transition back to peace, stability, good government and the preservation of the status quo. To do this it was necessary to consign the past to oblivion.

However, the past resists attempts to be forgotten or overlooked. Despite its attempts to erase many of those religious, social and political changes wrought during the Interregnum, and to pretend at a continuity of government from before the Civil Wars, the Restoration and the later Glorious Revolution did not find it so easy to put the genie back in the bottle. Despite the re-imposition of censorship, the re-establishment of the Church of England, and the introduction of the Clarendon Codes that obstructed the practice of dissenting Protestant beliefs, the general fear of Catholic plots and a resurgent Papism remained, and the non-conformism that had proliferated during the Republic continued.

Satan's Claw demonstrates this resistance by the past to be put out of sight and out of mind. Anxiety surrounding the cult in the film can be considered analogous, in many respects, to the fears of the late 17th and early 18th centuries surrounding the continuation of Protestant non-Conformist groups from the Commonwealth period, a time that saw 'a great overturning, questioning, revaluing, of everything in England' (Hill, 1978: 14), as well as the perennial concern about treacherous Catholic cells bent on overturning the Anglican government and Church. The cult in *Satan's Claw* bears some resemblance to these Non-Conformist sects in their repudiation of formal and traditional forms of worship, their self-removal from the community to set up their own separate commune, and the mutual antagonism held between them and society at large. Indeed, the cult shares some passing similarities to one sect in particular, the Ranters, who were considered to be a threat to moral order primarily because they embraced antinomianism, which holds that salvation is achieved purely through personal faith and divine grace and not through obedience to moral laws. As such, they advocated blasphemy as 'a symbolic expression of freedom from moral restraints' (Hill, 1978: 202) and held that sin was part of God's plan (and sinning in accordance with God's Will), as well as being frequently associated with nudity and accused of sexual immorality. The cult in *Satan's Claw* certainly demonstrates some Ranter-esque tendencies, including blasphemy through an inversion of Christian worship, a freedom to sin and indulge in behaviour proscribed by society, and ritual nudity.

The relationship between the cult and the wider community then expresses a tension at the time contemporary to when the film is set. The attempts during the Restoration and the remainder of the 17th century, to contain and roll back the changes rung in during the Civil Wars and the Commonwealth, were only partially successful: 'radicalism is never far away from Restoration' (Young, 2010: 17). There was a heightened paranoid fear of clandestine religious and political activities aimed at destabilising the state; the radical beliefs of the Ranters, and other sects like them as well as secret Catholics, were not thought of as being eradicated but instead had gone underground and continued to threaten the status quo.

Reviving forgotten horrors

The remains Ralph unearths are neither animal nor human: a half-buried skull with at least one intact eye, some fur, and a claw. The skull (also described simply as a face) vanishes: when Ralph takes the Judge to the field to see it, it has mysteriously disappeared, causing the Judge to doubt Ralph's story. The claw is not apparent at the start of the film when the other remains are uncovered. Instead it is found by Angel Blake in the same turned field when out playing with Mark and Cathy Vespers. It is, however, kept hidden from the viewer and only revealed two scenes later, when the children are at Bible study with the Reverend Fallowfield. In between the scenes of its discovery and reveal, Rosalind Barton is removed from the attic of the Banham house by men from Bedlam and in doing so it is revealed that her hand has become a claw.

The remains are curious. Despite appearing to catalyse the tragic train of events that unfold, they are completely inanimate – to all intents and purposes, they are the lifeless remains of a dead creature. While the skull contains an eye, it appears to stare sightlessly ahead (it does not, for example, rove about like that of a living thing). While its appearance may both repulse and unsettle (especially the fleshiness and intact eye, which are bizarre attributes for something long buried) the lack of either life or full corporeality would suggest that there is no danger from it, any more than there would be from any other unearthed, inanimate object. However, the skull's disappearance suggests a previously unexpected animacy, despite its apparent lifelessness. We next see it as part of the semi-reconstructed demon. The demon itself also performs none of the brutal activities that enable its resurrection – that is achieved by Angel and the cult she influences and leads. Despite its key role in initiating, and then driving, the savage tragedies we see, the remains and the demon are mostly absent from the film. While

Unearthing forgotten horrors © Tigon

the film's portmanteau origins are very likely betrayed by the peculiar behaviour of the remains and the fiend, the ambiguity and uncertainty surrounding them and their activities contributes to an effective disquieting atmosphere.

Not only are the demonic remains uncanny by virtue of their peculiar anatomy, they are also uncanny by virtue of being out of time. Their provenance is unknown, however they are clearly from some historic time, since buried and brought to the surface by the action of the plough, and possibly by some malign agency of the landscape itself. Even in costuming the fiend, there was the attempt to suggest an 'earthy, tree-rooted shape' (Haggard, 2019), something that looked like it had emerged from, and was part of, the natural wilderness. The remains, like the forest wilderness, hail from the same esoteric and immemorial past: a time impossible to define but one that stretches back before human activity and the presence of civilisation. Uncovered in the 18th century, a world turning away from superstition and towards reason, it is an anachronism. The fiend returns as a restored sprite or nature deity, once venerated in the wilderness before the settlement of the village and the encroachment of the cultivated fields, an old god becoming a new devil (Krzywinska, 2017). As such it is a relic from the periphery of civilisation as it is both from the immemorial past and from the natural wilderness – it is both anachronistic and anatopistic (out of place) emerging in a cultivated field in the 18th century.

The skull's unearthing represents the return of the repressed from an older and darker time, a presence that had literally been forced down into the earth itself to be forgotten and consigned to the past, until the physical barrier of the earth was breached and the skull is manifested as a relic from history. The earth itself is the material into which we try and banish those things we want to forget – because of trauma, guilt, secrecy, shame or greed – believing that once they are underground they will never return. The earth itself is implicated in the fiend's release and, like the rural landscape, it could be considered to be an active agent in the narrative, a geological sentience (Macfarlane, 2015).

The question of how and why the relic of the body of the devil came to be under a field in England is never resolved.[1] This lack of resolution and clarity suggests that the devil could return at any time and anywhere, especially as there was nothing special about the village and the community; their anonymity and nondescript appearance suggest how imminent evil is. There is an uneasiness that the devil could return anywhere and at any time – we must always be vigilant at it did not apparently require special circumstances or a ritual to return.

SCORING SATAN'S CLAW

This sense of anachronism and anatopism is echoed by Marc Wilkinson's musical score. While it can be problematic to discuss musical anachronism when considering period and historically set films (given that the vast majority of the scores for these films are composed, orchestrated and performed using techniques and technologies contemporary to the production, rather than the narrative) this does not mean that an exploration of the relationship between musical and narrative anachronisms is without merit, especially in films like *The Blood on Satan's Claw* where the concept of the anachronism is deeply rooted. Scovell identifies deliberate nods to the musical styles and forms popular in the early 1970s, particularly those associated with the cultural forms prevalent within the film, namely youth counter-culture, folk movements and pagan revivalism. These musical references can be heard in the use of a small ensemble rather than large orchestra for the score, the number of melodies led by flute, and the recurrent use of heavy percussion. There are instances of electronic modulation over analogue sounds, such as the distortion of the cymbal crash heard as Ralph uncovers the skull (Scovell, 'The music of folk horror, part 7'). Synthesised music would become commonplace from the 1980s onwards but was in its experimental phase in the 1960s and early 1970s and would have been considered avant-garde. The use of this modulated effect to signify the unearthing of the grim remains serves to highlight the uncanniness of the skull and its asynchronicity to the 18th century world it emerges into. The modulated cymbal is joined in the opening sequence by a number of other instruments working to create a sense of the uncanny and the disquieting: a descending woodwind sound, and a high, almost electronic, single repeated tone (ibid.). These effects were produced using an ondes Martenot, one of the earliest electronic musical instruments, invented in 1928, which produces high, quavering sounds, not dissimilar to those of the better known theremin. The sounds produced appear as dissonant to the 18th century world of the narrative as they do to the 1970s world of the film's production. Wilkinson's attention to the ondes Martenot is not unusual at a time when historic instruments were being 'rediscovered'. David Munrow in particular led a revival in Early Music and brought instruments such as the crumhorn and the shawm back into music-making, and his music features in the score for Ken Russell's *The Devils* (1971) (Young, 2010).

The dissonance of these sounds reinforces the dissonance of the uncovered remains, with the sounds of the descending woodwind mirroring Ralph's activities in the opening sequence; just as Ralph's actions plough downwards into the soil, so the notes descend downwards. The effect is to emphasise the subterranean, the ground and the soil itself. The introduction of the uncanny quavering sound draws our attention to the presence of something both anachronistic and anatopistic, something that does not belong, and implicitly associates that uncanny presence with the material earth. This sense of the anachronistic and anatopistic continues into the credits sequence with a title score clearly inflected by the work of Vaughan Williams and other quintessential British pastoral compositions. This is entirely apt, given Williams' interest in developing a corpus of British music distinct from the prevailing Germanic influences of the 19th century and his interest in traditional British folksongs. The interweaving of Williams-esque melodies evokes 'the aesthetics and traditions of the rural landscape and countryside' (ibid.), underlining the film's emphasis on the materiality of the earth and the soil. The counterpoints of the forlorn flute and the percussion, along with the continuation of the descending woodwind, temper the sweetness of the folk melodies with a sense of unease and apprehension carried through from the opening sequence.

UNEARTHING THE DEVIL

The remains are a form of anachronism that the Iranian philosopher and writer Reza Negarestani refers to as 'xenolithic artifacts' or 'inorganic demons' (Negarestani, 2008: 223). In the notes to his work of theory-fiction *Cyclonopedia, complicity with anonymous materials*, Negarestani makes reference to relics from the past that he characterises as 'xenolithic artifacts' (from 'xenolith', meaning 'foreign rock'). They are characterised by being made of inorganic materials (hence the other name for them – 'inorganic demons') such as stone, wood or bone ('inorganic' here being associated with the inanimate and uncanny as wood and bone are, of course, organic matter). They are:

> Autonomous, sentient and independent of human will, their existence is characterised by their forsaken status, immemorial slumber, and their provocatively exquisite forms. (ibid.)

This is an accurate description of the fiend's remains in *Satan's Claw*. It is an object that unsettles and instils fear as soon as it is unearthed; Ralph's disbelieving and horrified reaction to its discovery, coupled with Marc Wilkinson's sinister score played on the ondes Martenot, leaves the viewer in no doubt that this is a malevolent entity, abandoned within the earth and unearthed out of time. A woodcut of its face appears in the Doctor's magical tome (images created by art director Arnold Chapkis and based on 17th-century woodcuts), suggesting it is a revenant spirit and one known to be evil and associated with witchcraft and demonic practises (Haggard, 2019, *Touching the Devil*). With its apparent smirk and lone, worm infested eye, it is inarguably 'provocatively exquisite', an unforgettable image. Despite its apparent inanimacy, it exerts a baleful influence that indicates malignant purpose and intent. Even the mere act of Ralph observing the fiend's skull appears to catalyse it into (unseen) action; no specific act of removal from the ground, summoning spell or anything of that sort is needed.

Negarestani goes on to describe the 'vectors of contagion' (2008: 224) of these inorganic demons, based upon the completeness and the proximity of the artefact. First-class relics are those that exist in a complete state. Second-class relics are those that exist in broken up states, and which may require reassembly and restoration for the artefact to attain its full power and influence. Third-class relics are 'relics by contamination', in other words, from having been in contact with complete relics. The demonic remains are closest to the definition of second-class relics; they are fragmented upon discovery and reconstituted at some point during the film – unseen by the viewer – to create the half-resurrected fiend. There is a case to be made that the village adolescents, who have been in contact with the artifacts and thus sprout demonic fur for the fiend to harvest, are themselves third-class relics. Their contact with the remains brings them under its influence, leading to their transformation into living relics.

The appearance of xenolithic artifacts of all classes is frequent across British television from the late 1960s to the late 1970s. Notable examples are the whistle from *Whistle and I'll Come to You* (based on the MR James short story 'Oh, Whistle, and I'll Come to You my Lad', published in 1904), the crown of Anglia from *A Warning to the Curious* (1972, dir. Lawrence Gordon Clark, also based on an MR James' short story of the same name, published 1925), and the skull uncovered by scientists in the Doctor Who story *Image of the Fendahl* (1977, dir. George Spenton Foster). In all these instances the objects are implied to have rested in the earth for a considerable, and yet enigmatic, length of time. Unlike in the original short story (in which the whistle is located in a former Knight's Templar cemetery), in Jonathan Miller's 1968 adaptation, Professor Parkin happens across the whistle when he visits a local graveyard by the beach. There is no mention of the provenance of the whistle, or indeed the graveyard. It is clearly old, but its origins are kept obscure. The crown in *A Warning to the Curious* and the skull in *Image of the Fendahl* are objects from our Anglo-Saxon and prehistoric pasts respectively, however their exact temporal locations are not elaborated upon. The crown of Anglia is also the subject of local legend, while the skull in the *Doctor Who* story is that of an alien interloper into human development, so both stories interweave verifiable history with legend and diegetic fictions. The skull in *Satan's Claw* embodies that same sense of ambiguous antiquity. It is an object that is similarly opaque in terms of a specific and verifiable provenance. It is old, having been buried, but in an ill-defined and non-specific way. Its exact nature is ambiguous and uncanny: similar to the skull in *Image of the*

Fendahl, it is both a familiar remnant but has disconcertingly unfamiliar qualities (for the Fendahl skull, its apparently alien origins; for the *Satan's Claw* skull, its disturbing appearance as neither man nor beast but something approximating both). It is also, like the crown of Anglia, the embodiment of history and myth. The crown is a local legend, supposed to protect the country from invasion. Paxton's discovery of the crown, rather like Schliemann's excavation of Troy, gave it a veracity that moved it from a speculative legend to historical certainty. The discovery of the skull in *Satan's Claw* similarly authenticates a folk legend in the Doctor's book of witchcraft that is illustrated with a demonic image that bears a strong resemblance to the discovered skull.

Xenolithic artifacts, emerging as they do from the materiality of the landscape, exist in symbiotic relationship to that landscape and its topography. The crown of Anglia in *A Warning to the Curious* is established as the protector of the realm, physically embedded within the physical substance of the land over which it is guardian. Its removal from the earth brings down retribution upon the unwitting Paxton. In *Whistle and I'll Come to You*, the whistle appears to catalyse the appearance of an apparition that menaces Professor Parkin when he unearths and removes it. In *Stigma* (1977, dir. Lawrence Gordon Clark), another of the BBC's A Ghost Story for Christmas television plays, the removal of an ancient menhir uncovers the bones of a long deceased woman and unleashes a terrible a curse on one of the unsuspecting characters. There are commonalities shared between these objects and the remains uncovered in *Blood on Satan's Claw*: the separation of the object from the earth is (although the protagonists within the narratives are unaware of this at the time) undesirable. Firstly, the 'immemorial slumber' that marks these objects out as xenolithic artifacts is therefore implicitly considered to be the preferred state for these objects, and that they resent their awakening. Secondly, that the apparent wish for these objects to remain undisturbed and unearthed suggests a close and inextricable connection between them and the landscapes that surround them. Even when the xenolithic objects in question are not buried but are instead visible and notable landmarks – for example the stone circle in *Children of the Stones* (1977, dir. Peter Graham Scott) – they remain in contact with the earth and are as much a part of the topography of the landscape as those elements like hills and valleys that are composed of rock and soil. The unearthed remains of *Satan's Claw* demonstrate that same relationship with the landscape, and that same implicit resentment for being brought to the surface. Once unearthed, they appear to act upon that resentment and punish, or otherwise negatively affect, those individuals or communities who have contributed to their emergence (or even those who are simply in close proximity), supports Negarestani's characterisation of these artifacts as '[A]utonomous, sentient and independent of human will'.

THE FIEND AND THE LANDSCAPE

The fiend's unearthing from the cultivated landscape, and its occupation of the wilderness, illustrates how far it steps outside of the usual human relationships with the land. Where Ralph, Cathy and the other villagers are diminished by the scale and ubiquity of the rural landscape – their autonomy to operate within it restricted by notions of land use and occupation – the fiend appears to move freely, a freedom it grants to its cult who show no fear in occupying the forest or (in the case of Angel) appearing naked within the church. The fiend transgresses notions of ownership and function, moving freely between cultivated land, the wilderness and the farmhouse without care or consideration for social hierarchy or use of space. Civilisation and how it constructs meaning for itself through form, ownership, function and demarcation, are mocked by the devil's ability to move anywhere and inflict trauma. In doing so, the fiend degrades the values and structures of the status quo. As a result, nowhere feels safe or secure, and the countryside increasingly mocks its own supposed beauty and constancy.

The landscape of the fiend is one marked by repulsive objects, sites of abandonment, and savage behaviours. It effectively creates its own landscape to suit its purposes, an 'anti-landscape, the landscape that provocatively throws into question the very idea of the human/national subject as the owner of the landscape, as a figure in that landscape, or as an observer of it' (Hutchings, 2004: 29). The 'anti-landscape' of the film becomes one alive with past horror and present trauma, it is 'a realm that snags, bites and troubles' (Macfarlane, 2015).

The fiend's origination from the earth, a space traditionally gendered and anthropomorphicised as female and a mother, and away from the patriarchal socio-political structures of the status quo in the towns and cities, marks it as symbolic of the ancient and abject feminine. The relationship the fiend has with its followers – demarking their bodies with fur in different areas – is analogous to what Julia Kristeva and Barbara Creed have identified as the mother's instrumental role in mapping the infant body during childhood, zoning the body into clean and unclean areas. Where the mother zones the infant body to identify and remove the uncleanliness, the fiend does the opposite: its actions are to create areas of unclean fur and remove the areas of cleanliness. The violent giving of the devil's skin – through murder and mutilation – then functions not only as abject in itself (inextricably associated as it is with blood and gore and in its affront to the laws of the patriarchal status quo) but also as a ritual expulsion of the abject. The return of the demon from the subterranean space can be interpreted as symbolic of the return of the primeval maternal authority following its repression by the more masculine forces of reason, rationality and structure represented in the film by the Judge. The assertion of the demon, its emergence and the formation of its worshipping cult that revels in those abject materials and behaviours cast out by the masculine status quo, demonstrates the fragility of the patriarchal status quo, its laws and structures. Its awakening, from beneath the very land we walk and cultivate for our sustenance and survival, tells us that our abject selves remain hidden at our horizons. As Creed states in relation to *The Exorcist* (1973, dir. William Friedkin), but relevant to *Satan's Claw*, the abject 'can never be successfully obliterated but lie in wait at the threshold of the subject's identity, threatening it with possible breakdown' (Creed, 2007: 40). The subjects are the village, the wider status quo of Early Modern England in the film and, implicitly, also the world of the viewer.

THE CONTINUITY OF PAGAN WORSHIP

The unearthing of the fiend sees a restored form of pre-Christian, and possibly pre-civilisation, worship in the sacred wilderness. *The Blood on Satan's Claw* was one of many novels, films and television shows of the 1960s and 1970s that addressed the revival or continuation of pagan beliefs into modern (or in this case Early Modern) times. A notable contributing factor to this flurry of interest in Britain's pagan and quasi-mythical past was the reprinting in 1962 of Margaret Murray's influential 1921 book *The Witch-Cult in Western Europe*. While Murray's argument has been discredited, it proved remarkably influential on witchcraft and Satanism in popular culture in Britain. Murray contended that evidence from the late Mediaeval and Early Modern periods – trial records, pamphlets, accounts by inquisitors and other writers – pointed to the existence of a pagan cult, one that predated Christianity and continued to operate beneath it for centuries. While this cult permeated across all societies, it was most prevalent among the poorly educated classes in the more sparsely populated parts of the country. Murray argued that this was an organised, defined religion with specific rituals, and one that existed across the whole of Western Europe. The god worshipped by this cult took a variety of forms – man, woman, animal, two-faced man – and was often depicted as a horned god. Murray contended that the Christian authorities, when they came across the cult, mistook the horned god for Satan and that the witch-cult was satanic and duly persecuted the witches and stamped their activities out.

The Blood on Satan's Claw betrays the influence of Murray's beliefs in this witch-cult and its rituals. The village in Satan's Claw is exactly the sort of community that Murray identifies as where the witch-cult would thrive: a sparsely populated, isolated and remote community. Murray stated that the conversion of Britain to Christianity was initially a conversion of the elites, and that it took far, far longer for the people to adopt Christianity. They instead would continue to worship the old religion under a 'veneer of Christian rites' (Murray, 1963: 19). Over time, as Christianity permeated further into society and built its own structures and authorities, it created and implemented injunctions against heathen rites and practises, or in some cases assimilated and absorbed some of the rites (Murray cites may-pole dancing as an example). The village in the film highlights how folkloric and residual heathen belief co-exist with Christianity. While the Reverend Fallowfield leads Bible study for the village youth, the local Doctor focuses on folkloric medicine and consults a tome of magic, and there are suggestions that occurrences of witchcraft are not unknown in the area (Fallowfield's allusion to a person called Meg Parsons is made in connection with odd occurrences and unusual strangers). They appear to exist comfortably alongside each other in this rural outpost. Murray suggests that the witch-cult had a structured hierarchy built around a series of linked but independent cultic groups, and it is a structure that has informed our popular image of the witches' coven or the satanic church that can be seen in The Witches and The Devil Rides Out. The witch-cult in Satan's Claw shares similarities with Murray's

Ritualised sacrifice in communion with nature © Tigon

description. There is a discrete circle of individuals who meet at a designated sacred place and enact their rituals. These rituals are led by a senior minister, in this case Angel, in an apparent parody of Christian worship (although Murray would maintain that the cult's organisation and ritual predate Christianity, and in fact it is Christianity that has been shaped by the witch-cult and not vice-versa). Angel clearly occupies the senior position in the group, anointing Cathy with a crown of hawthorn, presiding over her ritualised rape, and carrying out herself her sacrificial killing. The rest of the group clearly defer to her, and she seems to have a special and intimate relationship with the fiend. However, there are some differences to Murray's witch-cult organisation, the most critical being the lack of overt consistency and structure. While the group does have its rituals, chants and a holy text, there appears to be little that is prescribed or regular about their rituals; during Cathy's assault and murder the group seems unsure and hesitant, albeit thrilled and excited, about the direction the ritual will take. The viewer understands that the ritual will culminate most likely in Cathy's death, having seen her brother murdered earlier, however we do not know the form this will take. The viewer is almost complicit in the same anticipatory uncertainty. In her book Murray identifies that the cult had elaborate admission ceremonies, marked by singing and dancing, and this is evident in the film. Cathy's approach to the sacred ruins, her assault and murder are all highly ritualised. While it culminates in her sacrifice, it arguably also functions as an admission ceremony as she is crowned and greeted with great celebration as she is led to the ruins. Singing and dancing are also key features of the final scene as a background ritual to Ralph's imminent sacrificial mutilation.

Murray's opinion that this pre-Christian witch-cult was primarily a fertility cult and one linked explicitly with nature, is clearly influential on the representation of the cult in *Satan's Claw*. The cult operates and carries out its rituals in the ruins in the middle of woods, at the heart of the wilderness and far from the village. The ruins also express a form of worship in communion with nature, as opposed to the enclosed buildings of the Church. Murray identified an influential connection between the figure of the female cult leader (represented in the film by Angel) and the legendary figure of the Queen of the Faeries/Elfin Queen. While such an association is at best obscure, it is another link between the operation of the cult and the more mystical aspect of nature. Of course, the feature of fertility worship that the film most embraces (in common with much film, television and literature with an interest in witchcraft and Satanism), and an aspect that caused Murray some chagrin, is the sexual rites. Murray (1963) asserts that this aspect of the rituals has received far more notoriety that it deserves, and that this functioned more as ceremonial magic than some sort of bacchanalian orgy. However, most media chose to interpret this perception of witchcraft through a more titillating prism and *Satan's Claw* is no exception. The worship of the fiend in the film is associated with transgressive sexual activity. Not only is Cathy raped, but she is raped by a male cult member who appears to bear a striking resemblance to her deceased brother (the moderator of the 2019 audio commentary explicitly identifies this figure as a restored Mark Vespers), inflecting the assault with incestuous undertones. Cathy's murder immediately following her violation implicitly associates the sexual fluids of Cathy and the youth who rapes her with blood and then, when Angel licks the bloodied shears, with saliva too; a trespassing of the abject that offends civilised values. The cult's behaviour is also associated with the more liberal, permissive attitudes of the late 1960s (this will be explored in more depth in the last chapter), both critiquing this form of expression whilst also creating commercially focused opportunities to titillate the audience: both Angel and one of the female youths in the cult appear fully nude. There is an explicit connection made between the values of the 1960s hippy counter-culture, nature worship, witchcraft, and permissive behaviours, although this is not unusual of the late sixties and early seventies.

The absolute devotion Murray asserts the witch-cult had for their horned god – a figure they did not, according to her, associate with the devil but instead worshipped as their own deity – is clear in *Satan's Claw*, particularly in the figure of Margaret. Were it not for the sexualised and brutal nature of the cult's rituals, Margaret's fervency and reverence for the fiend, and her absolute, unshakeable faith in him, is akin to the fervour of Christian martyrs and that she maintains her beliefs even under threat of torture. Indeed, there are aspects of the film that were included purely to reflect this Murray-inflected perspective of witchcraft because our popular image of such things requires them to be there. The scene in which Margaret is ducked in the lake, for example, was at the request of the producers, as ducking witches is an activity they felt the audience would know and would expect (following the inclusion of a similar scene in *Witchfinder General*). The ducking of Margaret finds its basis in the Mediaeval punishment of Ordeal by Water in which the witch was bound crossways (right thumb to left big toe; left thumb to right big toe) and cast into the water, and where sinking indicated innocence of the crime and floating indicated guilt.

ANGEL BLAKE

Linda Hayden's Angel dominates the film, despite a surprising lack of screen time. Angel Blake is, in the general absence of the corporeal demon, our key antagonist. We only have one scene with her in, where she is playing in the ploughed field with Mark and Cathy Vespers, before she is affected by the diabolical remains. The scene we see of her shortly afterwards – in the school room in the church – shows her already attempting to conceal the claw as a precious and secret totem from the eyes of the Reverend Fallowfield. The next time we actually see Angel she is leading the cult and killing Mark Vespers. It is a remarkably speedy transition. Arguably, as we only see Angel in one scene before her 'possession' by the demon, it makes it problematic to assess just how far she is affected by it. In her first scene she is playing more with Mark than with Cathy, who seems to be there more because her brother is there than because she is interested in playing. Mark's focus is entirely on Angel, on whom he has a very obvious crush, something she is aware of and clearly enjoys. On introduction then, Angel is spirited, flirtatious, aware of her own sexuality and the power that it can have, and is clearly used to leading rather than following. Of these three, Angel's' association with the demonic power is perhaps, then, inevitable, certainly in comparison to Cathy (who would be too pious to be drawn to it) and Mark (who would be too timid). We see her fascination with the claw in her efforts to hide it from the Curate. It begins as an attempt to conceal an illicit toy – very much the sort of thing naughty school children might do. In another context it could be played for comedic value, however here it becomes something far darker and crueller – an attempt to embarrass Reverend Fallowfield. Later, we see the humiliation of the Curate taken to a greater level. Angel's move from child to adult is accelerated and manipulated by the demon. Her spiritedness and wilfulness are not only magnified but influenced towards malevolence.

Angel's relationship with the demon is never made clear. She appears to lead and direct the children independently of the demon; in the earlier part of the film, the children defer to her rather than to it. For example, when Mark is lured away by the two girls, or when Margaret attempts to seduce Ralph, mention is made specifically of Angel rather than the fiend. At other points the demon is mentioned as the source of power; Margaret in particular makes many references to her 'master'. On occasion, Angel behaves as if she is either possessed by, or able to channel and manipulate, the demon's power; at Mark's burial for example, by staring intently at Cathy she seems to will the devil's fur into existence on her back. Yet at other times she appears to be the devil's equal. Shortly before the final confrontation at the film's climax she stands alongside the demon almost as peers. Indeed, their closeness to each other in this scene almost identifies them as a couple. Often, Angel appears to take on the agency of the demon, as the demon appears to have no agency of its own. As such, it is ambiguous as to how far the demon and Angel are separate entities or conjoined in some way.

Angel becomes a representation for the abject within the film. She is an adolescent at an age of sexual maturation, and one aware of her emergent sexuality and the power it has. There is a compelling association within Angel between the repulsive – in terms of her involvement in rape and murder – and the attractive, in terms of her beauty and sexuality. Unlike, for example, young Regan in The Exorcist, who is a pubescent, innocent girl, Angel is depicted as flirtatious and sexually knowing from her first scene. Where the abject boundary traversed is usually between innocence and corruption – in The Exorcist the slow corruption of Regan's innocence and the gradual abjection of her body

– the notion of a similar boundary being transgressed in *Satan's Claw* is opaque. Where Regan's body is forcibly occupied by the demon Pazuzu, her innocence defiled and her soul transformed into a battleground for the self to assert authority and expel the abject, there are no such clear lines in the relationship between Angel and the demon. Where Regan's purity seemingly invites Pazuzu with the irresistible temptation for despoilation, Angel's worldliness identifies her as a co-conspirator with the demon and they operate in a malign synergy. Unlike Regan, who is to be purged of the abject and saved, Angel is never considered to be in need of saving or redeeming; she is expunged alongside the demon without guilt or regret.

It is Angel rather than the demon, who takes on the role of directing the activities of the cult. Her visible authority in summoning away the village children (and some villagers – not all of the cult members are children; there is a minority of older cult members too) from the socio-political structures of the village to establish a new hierarchy of power in the wilderness directly challenges the patriarchal authority represented in the film by the Judge, Peter Edmonton, the Curate, the Squire and the Doctor. She forms a new, separate society, beyond the bounds of civilisation, but one that is inimical and threatening to civilisation, consuming it to expand and grow. Angel, therefore, as a social leader, transgresses traditional gender roles and usurps the masculine function. She functions as a female Squire by meting out punishment and keeping order within the cult; for example, when she punishes Margaret for her perceived duplicity. She functions as female Curate by leading the cult rituals and acting as mediator and interlocutor between the demon and its congregation. And she acts as female Doctor through her apparent power to affect the physical bodies of the cult members and to use those to recreate the demon. Angel also undertakes the function of the Judge, who returns to issue rough justice through 'undreamed of measures', by similarly orchestrating activities whose brutality would not have been conceivable to the locals.

Angel appears to simultaneously occupy a number of monstrously feminine aspects. She is the possessed monster, mediating the demon's power across the cult. Her relationship with the demon inspires a bloodlust and a fixation on the abject materials of the body – witness her sexually charged licking of Cathy's blood from shears. Angel represents the abject in that she 'disturbs identity, system, order' (Kristeva, 1982), the system and order of the patriarchal establishment of law, society, religion and science as represented by the male authority figures we see in the film. Discussion of abjection posits the abject as feminine in opposition to the 'masculine symbolic', which is governed by law and rules. This opposition is at the heart of *Satan's Claw*, a cult of predominantly children led by an adolescent woman (Angel) in which another adolescent woman (Margaret) has an instrumental role in speaking the litany and that situates itself in the wilderness – the immemorial home of pre-civilisation – in direct contrast to the male-dominated world of the village and London, places defined by rules and laws created and maintained by the patriarchal status quo.

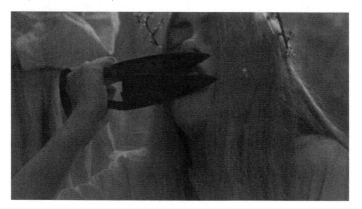

Abject desires – Angel as the monstrous feminine © Tigon

For the majority of the film, the abject fixation on the body and its matter is located within the feminine cult, a clear association between the feminine, the physical body and abject assaults upon it (rape, mutilation, murder), and substances that come from it (blood and viscera). For full acceptance into the sphere of patriarchal order, all forms of 'unacceptable, improper or unclean' speech, action and behaviour must be either repressed or rejected (Creed, 2007: 37). In particular, it is those associations with the abject matter of infantile bodily experiences – blood, mucus, urine and faeces – that must be rejected and expelled. It is then very telling that the cult comprises mostly children (with a visible minority of the elderly) and that it is presided over by female adolescents. There are clear associations between those abject materials of the body and both the young and the old (in terms of infancy and 'second childhood' in which our control over the proper expulsion of abject material, and our understanding of this material as abject and in need of expulsion, are not fully comprehended) as well as during pubescent adolescence; in particular there are clear connections made between a number of abject activities and states: the sexual delight derived by Angel and Margaret at Cathy's stabbing, the act of bloodletting itself, and their status as pubescent and very likely menstrual adolescent females. Cathy's rape also highlights another abject material of adolescence, that of semen. Cathy's murder identifies a further transgression of abject boundaries. Despite Angel's assertion of an abject, feminine authority in direct opposition to the patriarchal status quo, her fundamental act (and arguably the most critical point of the whole film) is the absolute destruction of another female (Cathy), rather than a man. Mark is lured and murdered first, but his abduction serves to build tension for Cathy's subsequent ensnaring, and his actual death occurs off-screen. The point at which he is throttled is quick, designed to shock the apprehensive viewer. In contrast Cathy's murder is one of the longest sequences in the film, uncomfortably drawn out through the ritual and the litany to build the dread and foreboding. Angel's presiding over the rape of Cathy, and then her instrumental role in stabbing her with the shears identifies her in an overtly threatening masculine, rather than feminine, authority. The shears offer a clearly phallic image as Angel plunges them relentlessly into Cathy, pausing only to lick her blood from the blades. Angel then, occupies both the monstrous feminine and monstrous masculine space, a transgression of social and gendered roles that could also be described as abject.

The abject is a state associated with the archaic, the same ambiguous antiquity from whence the fiend originates, and represents a point at which an understanding of physical boundaries coalesces. It is fitting to describe the relationship between the members of the cult and the fiend as abject. The corporeality of the cult members, and their sense of individuality and agency, is degraded in that they are used to physically reproduce the form of the demon. Not only is this abject in terms of the apparently spontaneous growth of fur on the bodies of the youths – an incongruous presence on the human form, its association with animals aligning it with the bestial and primitive – but also in the co-existence of two entities in one physical form; they are as much the fiend as they are their individual selves. Given the abject bodies of the young cult members, and the compromised state of their sense of self, it is perhaps understandable that they then regress to savage behaviours that challenge each other's corporeal boundaries, such as rape and mutilation.

Angel is not only monstrous from the aspect of possible possession by the demon, but also in her role as witch. The cult of the children is not unlike that of a coven, meeting in the wilderness away from the prying eyes of the village to conduct ceremonies that would be considered offensive to established values and beliefs. Angel acts very much as the senior witch, leading a coven in the worship of the devil. The sprouting of fur across the children – the resurgence and rebellion of the abject body – is analogous to the supposed witch's teat, the third nipple that the *Malleus Maleficarum* (1484) – the 15th-century text on the identification, trial and punishment of witches – suggested exists for the witch to suckle her familiars and even the devil. Like the teat, the fur in the film indicates that Angel and the cult exist to nourish the demon, to provide the sustenance needed for it to build its strength and vigour. The oft-made accusation that witches enjoyed a sexual relationship with the devil is hinted at broadly across *Satan's Claw* in the relationship between Angel and the demon. Not only is she chosen as the cult leader but her closeness and proximity to it in the last scene of the film – plus their consecutive deaths at the hands of the mob – are suggestive of some sort of close relationship. Indeed, it is in this last sequence that Wynne-Simmons intended to imply Angel giving oral sex to the demon, an implication almost invisible due to an abrupt cut as Angel begins to drop down in front of the fiend. The ambiguity around Angel's relationship with the demon might suggest powers it has bestowed on her, rather than his powers possessing and working through her. For example, like a witch, she appears to be able to inflict harm on others by supernatural means: at Mark's funeral, her intense stare, accompanied by threatening music in the score, is focused on Cathy. Cathy becomes aware of Angel staring at her, and then doubles over in pain. In the following scene, as she returns home with her mother and Ralph, she makes mention of a pain across her back. During the rape scene, as her clothes are torn from her, we see that a patch of the devil's skin has grown across the part of her back that Angel was staring at so intently. Indeed, throughout the film, eyes are closely associated with malign power. The opening sequence concludes with an extreme close-up of the skull's eye followed by a close-up of Ralph's expression of fear and disgust. Later, during Mark's funeral, a close-up of Angel's eyes, accompanied by a musical crescendo, indicates she is focusing the fiend's malevolent power at Cathy. She returns Angel's gaze with fear, a parallel to the exchange between the skull and Ralph at the start of the film. Of course, there is a similar scene that concludes the film, as the Judge's eye peers through the fire in freeze-frame, gazing into the middle distance. There is no one to return the Judge's gaze, but it is suggestive that he has somehow become an agent of the fiend's malign power.

THE CHILDREN AND THE CULT

A key concern of *The Blood on Satan's Claw* is the corruption of childhood innocence, and the idea that children are innately evil and have the capacity to commit acts of brutality. Throughout the film, the narrative plays with the notion of playfulness and barbarity. Childhood, rather like the rural landscape, is an uncanny and troubled space that can be both serene and malign.

Towards the beginning of the film we see the village children engaged in activities that would have been part of their everyday life – playing in the fields, respecting and responding to their elders, attending Bible study led by the local priest. It is a continuation of the opening sequence in which we are given a glimpse into the constancy and normality of rural life and how the rural is an integral part of existence (the fields as a playground for Mark, Cathy and Angel, for example). There is the sense of a contentment with the seamlessness of moving from children who play in the fields to adults who plough those same fields, on and on ad inifinitum. However, as the unearthing of the remains quickly destabilises these notions of tranquillity, constancy and security within the rural landscape, so Angel's fixation on the claw does the same for the same notions of childhood. Their childish antics during Bible study are inflected with a spite and cruelty that clearly unnerves the Curate. These scenes demonstrate the awkward tension between childhood innocence and a state of a lack of innocence that is not yet adulthood.

Mark, like Angel, is clearly undergoing a period of sexual awakening, and his 'leading away' – where he is approached in his home by two girls who tell him Angel wants to play with him – is a clear example of this. This sequence even begins with Mark playing knucklebones as if to underline the change from childhood pleasures to adult ones. Playing, while initially innocent, becomes a metaphor for sexuality, especially as it is the idea of playing with Angel that tempts him to his doom. Later, Margaret will attempt to lead Ralph away with similar suggestions of playing and 'lying with' that leave no doubt as to the meaning. There is also the metaphor for playing as acts of violence. Mark's death scene begins with a game of Blind Man's Bluff, making explicit reference to Mark's lack of foresight and awareness that his actions are leading to his imminent death. The free-moving, hand-held camera in this scene is a good example of Dick Bush's attempts to try new ways of filming. The effect is accomplished and makes the viewer complicit as a member of the cult. It creates a disturbing intimacy and uneasiness as the children suddenly stop playing and fall back. The camera moves round to face Mark, framed in the stone threshold of the ruins with the silent and immobile children behind him. Suddenly a vine is thrown round his neck as Angel throttles him. Angel is positioned behind the camera at this point and the positioning once again makes the viewer complicit, only this time it is in Mark's murder rather than in the game.

Dangerous games and the perversion of play © Tigon

Mark's death, rather than sexual awakening, at the hands of Angel, only serves to further reinforce the troubling associations between play, sex and death in the film. That she appears to strangle him with a vine, makes explicit the connection with nature, and by extension the association between the primitive, natural wilderness with sex and violence as modes of creation rather than destruction. The acts of destruction – the murders of Mark and Cathy, the mutilation of the cultists through the removal of the fiend's fur – become acts of creation in that they are necessary to restore the demon.

It is telling that when the game transitions to something more sinister the children fall back as passive observers, unsure of what to do in this scenario. They will show no such passivity when Cathy is raped and murdered, illustrating the incremental loss of their innocence, and their increasing comfort in the adult games of violent behaviour. However, the sequence of Cathy's assault and murder also begins with a game and with children at play, although this game is inflected with sense of menace and foreboding from the outset:

> She is led away through empty fields, through forests and pastures, as if playing in some Enid Blyton jaunt; an innocent game that ignores the gradual journey towards a more isolated location. (Scovell, 2017: 21)

Cathy's luring away is more troubled than that of her brother. The two boys who approach her use a mix of play, threats, cajoling, wheedling, and violence to urge her on. Cathy moves from an open clearing in the woods (a beautiful image, framed within occlusive foliage that suggests at a clandestine voyeurism, and reminiscent of a very similar sequence in Bergman's *The Virgin Spring*), a locale that seems peaceful and serene. The boys lure her deep into the woods; the undergrowth becomes denser and their efforts become more aggressive. Cathy is moved, both physically and symbolically from a place of safety within the range of the village and its attendant security, to the heart of the wilderness where the status quo cannot protect her. The threat she is facing is underscored by the frequent and sharp cuts across to Ralph searching for her, heightening the sense that Cathy is in need of rescue.

The choreography of the cult, as they move from the two boys who lure Cathy with a mix of playfulness and menace, to the group who joyfully see her crowned with hawthorn, and then the eerie formality of their procession into the mist-bound ruins, gives it a memorable range of movement as well as a sense of dreadful uncertainty and a feeling of 'occult authenticity' (Sharp quoted in Beem and Paciorek (eds), 2015: 403). The May-flowering hawthorn has several folkloric and mythological associations. The ancient Greeks held that it was sacred to the marriage god Hymenaios; it decorated his altars and was used during marriage processions. In Gaelic folklore the hawthorn is associated with faeries and marks the entrance to the Otherworld. It was also believed to be the tree from which Jesus' Crown of Thorns was made. The flowering of the tree in May also gives rise to its associations with the Celtic festival of Beltane and the marking of the start of summer. When Haggard was recceing the locations, the trees had not yet budded. On returning for the shoot in the spring, the May blossom was coming into bloom. He noticed the hawthorn driving to the location one day and it occurred to him that, with its mixture of beautiful blossom and dangerous thorns, it could be incorporated into the sequence of Cathy's rape and murder to add a note of pagan ritualism. As someone who grew up in the countryside, Haggard would have been familiar with the sight of hawthorn, and very likely familiar with some of the folk tales associated with it: 'One did a bit of research ... but I didn't worry about, sort of, inventing it because you know what it would have been like' (Haggard, 2019). Thus it is a mix of research, common knowledge, folk tale and customs that inform the symbolism and presence of the hawthorn in the film.

The chanting, like the use of the hawthorn, was improvised by Haggard on the day of the shot. Despite the transgressive act of rape and intimations of incest, the scene is set up with distinctly matrimonial overtones: the procession has the feel of a wedding march, Cathy crowned symbolically like a bride, and she is laid down on a wooden frame for the violation, like a perverse marital bed (Sharp, 2015: 405). Cathy's rape and murder sees the children firmly set aside their childhood games; from here on play will be associated only with adult games of sex and death. Their initial passivity and perhaps incomprehension at Mark's murder, give away to positive delight at the new 'games' that Cathy is forced to be the subject of. They take a wilfully active role in holding Cathy down, tearing her clothes, and stabbing her, while those not participating actively and purposefully enjoy the violation.

FOOTNOTES

1. Robert Wynne-Simmons points out that the fiend was not intended to be *the* Devil but rather *a* devil as the film's focus was 'about an ancient religion, not necessarily Satanism' (Hamilton, 2005: 183)

AGENTS OF ORDER

Over the course of the film, we see a movement from order to disorder. The unearthing of the remains catalyses a train of corruption, rape and murder that exposes the impotence and frailties of local sources of justice, authority and knowledge. Arguably this is nothing unusual in horror cinema, where there is frequently a move from order to disorder and then back to order again. Andrew Tudor (1989) describes this narrative form as 'secure', and argues that it was the prevalent form up until the 1960s. Hammer Studios provides useful contemporary examples of this narrative form. *Dracula*, *The Mummy* (1959, dir. Terence Fisher) and *The Gorgon* (1964, dir. Terence Fisher) to pick three such examples all share features common to secure narratives: a bourgeois status quo is threatened by an exotic otherworldly threat – usually either implicitly or explicitly identified as something foreign and irrational – that is inimical to its health and vitality. The establishment is imperilled but saved by the actions of a hero who embodies the values of the status quo, invariably a man and usually of professional, middle-class standing. The films conclude with the threats unambiguously vanquished, and the establishment ultimately revivified and celebrated through its assailment and survival.

Tudor, though, identifies from 1960 onwards the increasing prevalence of narratives he describes as 'paranoid', rather than secure. In paranoid narratives, the status quo is threatened, not by some external and foreign force, but instead by an antagonist that originates from within. Usually this antagonist represents the status quo itself, and its emergence undermines not only the credibility of established authority and tarnishes those values associated with it, but also suggests that the status quo is actually not worth defending. Paranoid narratives rarely conclude with the explicit and wholesale defeat of the threat, and if they do, there is no valedictory triumph for the establishment. *The Blood on Satan's Claw* follows the pattern of the paranoid narrative. Established social structures are presented to us at the beginning of the film that are then threatened both by the fiend and its witch-cult, and by the retaliatory actions of the Judge. The remains may appear to be an external threat; they represent something from the supernatural, pagan, esoteric past, potentially as remote and exotic as if they had come from a spatially foreign period rather than a temporal one. However, they are unearthed from the village fields, from the English soil itself. They literally emerge from the green

Lingering unease – the fiend may be dead but does its influence live on? © Tigon

and pleasant lands that sustain the cultural perception of what England is, certainly as much as the manorial status quo we see as the established structure of authority within the film. The Judge too is part of this status quo, a representative of correct law and authority, deferred to by all. After a series of ordeals, the community, led with fire and brimstone zeal by the Judge confronts and apparently defeats the baleful influence of the demon. However, the ending is far less resolute and incontrovertible than those of the Hammer film examples. The credits playing over a frozen close-up of the Judge's eye, mirroring the film's opening close-up of the demon's worm-infested eye leering up from the ground, suggests a lingering unease and a less-than-total victory. The final freeze-frame also suggests a need for ceaseless watchfulness against the almost certain return of this malevolence from within those social and political structures that define our society. The freeze-frames at the end and the move to slow-motion were always intended by Haggard to imply that the malevolence still existed and could return. The ending implicitly acknowledges that this capacity for evil is part of our nature and cannot be hidden, buried or abandoned. We can never be victorious against it, only vigilant for its return. In many ways *The Blood on Satan's Claw* anticipates the films of Pete Walker, like *House of Whipcord* (1974) and *House of Mortal Sin* (1976). Certainly, it has more in common with them than it does with Hammer's horror, despite the period setting. Steve Chibnall identifies in *The Blood on Satan's Claw* the same pessimism and moral ambivalence that characterises Walker's films, as it 'struggles to find virtue in either its

Satanic youth cult or the cult's nemesis, the bigoted and domineering Judge' (Chibnall, 2002: 160). This chapter will address the problematic nature of authority in the film through an examination of the principal agents of order in the film: the Judge, the Squire, the Curate and the Doctor.

THE JUDGE

It can be argued that the Judge functions as the film's hero character in that he kills the demon and ends the influence and activities of the murderous cult, restoring the status quo to the village. However, it is problematic to define him so simplistically. The problem of the Judge is best explored through several prisms: as a professionalised individual, as an Enlightened thinker, and as a Jacobite supporter.

The professionalised Judge

Peter Hutchings identifies within Hammer's formative gothic horror films, principally those from 1957 to around 1964, an emphasis on the male professional figure. Hutchings perceives the character of Professor Quatermass – lead character in Hammer's first horror hits, *The Quatermass Xperiment* (1955, dir. Val Guest) and *Quatermass 2* (1957, dir. Val Guest) – as the template for this character trope. He argues that this template is then used for the leading male characters in some of Hammer's earliest gothic horror hits, such as Van Helsing, Baron Frankenstein and Sherlock Holmes. Hutchings argues that this focus on the professional as hero mirrors the social and political milieu from the late 1950s onwards. By the mid-1960s there was a contemporary cultural tension between the relative merits within British society of the amateur and the professional. At the Labour Party conference of 1963, Labour leader and soon-to-be Prime Minister Harold Wilson made his celebrated speech about the need to forge a new Britain in the white heat of technology, a vision of success and prosperity founded through scientific modernity and managerial efficiency. When his party came to power the following year, his government put this modernising agenda into effect focusing on education, industry, urban planning and economic growth. Hutchings sees Hammer and their body of professionalised male hero characters as tapping into this political desire to forge a modern, efficient, ordered Britain, part of what he described as the 'valorisation of professional activity' (Hutchings, 1993: 64). In contrast to the upper and lower classes in Hammer films – who are generally portrayed as parasitic or weak, and as ignorant or powerless respectively – the bourgeois professional is autonomous and empowered by virtue of his confidence, self-discipline and personal strength. These characters are invariably older men of means, usually of the middle- or upper-middle-class, and function as paragons of masculine authority, rationality and virtues like fortitude, abstemiousness and honour.

The Judge is interesting to compare to these professionalised Hammer heroes. In many respects he is a very similar character. Like Van Helsing and Holmes it is implicitly suggested that he is a celibate character (the only reference to any marital or love life to speak of is his passing mention that he was once a suitor to Isobel Banham). He is clearly professional; indeed, he is referred to by his professional title throughout the film in the absence of any name being given. He is a man of standing, substance and education, very likely a member of the gentry. He is an urban, rather than rural, dweller, and he places great emphasis on learning and rational thought, frequently castigating the villagers for their superstitious beliefs. His position affords him independence and autonomy. He is a man of great personal strength and confidence and displays a tremendous physicality – holding the demon aloft on his cross/sword, the phallic symbolism of which is a clear riposte by the patriarchal status quo to the fiend's female-led witch-cult.

However, despite these apparent similarities to the Hammer professionals, there are a greater number of differences that make it troublesome to identify the Judge as a heroic character. Firstly, as previous discussed, the context of the film is different to Hammer's. Where the professionalised male leads of Hammer's films operated in a universe of binary moral absolutes, the paranoid narrative of *Satan's Claw* is one of moral ambiguities. As such, the Judge cannot be so easily aligned to a clear and explicit righteousness and rectitude as can the likes of Van Helsing and Holmes. It is also difficult to recognise the same middle-class, bourgeois virtues in the Judge as can be seen in Hammer's leads. For example, while Van Helsing and Holmes are active and uncompromising in rooting out the evil in their midst, they are also measured, thoughtful, disciplined and compassionate. The Judge displays few of these traits. From his initial interactions with Ralph at the start of the film, he is generally dismissive of the villagers. His treatment of Peter and Rosalind is positively tyrannical; despite his position as a guest at the Banham house and not the master, he bullies the young people by assisting in Rosalind's imprisonment and assaulting Peter. The Judge could not be described as an especially compassionate character; he and Isobel clearly enjoy Peter and Rosalind's discomfort when they goad and tease them. Much later, the zeal with which he pursues and destroys the cult demonstrates precious little sympathy or concern for the youngsters. The Judge demonstrates no such considerations in separating the evil antagonist from those who may be in their thrall. In fact, he appears to relish the opportunity for wanton and widespread human devastation, advising the Squire and Ralph shortly before his departure for London to 'have patience, even while people die. Only thus can the whole evil be destroyed. You must let it grow.' His return towards the end of the film sees him resolved to use 'undreamed of measures' to root out the evil that has been allowed, under his entreaty, to grow and take hold of the community. The original ending that Robert Wynne-Simmons had in mind was far bleaker, and far more overt in identifying the Judge as an ambiguous and problematic character:

> Patrick Wymark had militiamen with him who actually gunned people down. There was a mass grave dug and that was the end. So it was really a very, very destructive thing. Rough justice, where he just obliterated this crowd of people. (Wynne-Simmons quoted in Taylor, 1996: 89)

Tigon executives were keen the Judge's behaviour be far closer to that of Peter Cushing's Van Helsing, hence the peculiarity in tone with the Judge's character, sitting awkwardly in the finished film as a morally ambiguous anti-hero. However, the ending-as–filmed still refuses to entertain the notion of the Judge as a heroic protagonist, despite his defeat of the demon. As Wynne-Simmons says 'the close-up of his eye at the end rather suggests he is now the devil himself' (ibid.). This equation between the demon and the Judge places him at odds to the professionalised leads of Hammer. The moral ambiguity of the Judge, however, does by extension, render the status quo he represents as morally ambiguous too. There is no sense that his world view is innately good or correct, nor that the restored status quo is either.

The Enlightened Judge

The Judge is the embodiment of what Wynne-Simmons calls 'a dogged enlightenment' (Wynne-Simmons quoted in Taylor, 1996: 88), the voice of the Age of Reason in the film, the intrusion of urban, modern and progressive Enlightenment thought. The Judge's philosophy is an empirical one, grounded in the measurable and observable universe. It is understandable that, for him, the evil needs to materialise into something physical, so that actions can be witnessed and experienced. For him it is only after the activities and effects of the evil can be testified to, corroborated and considered that it can be opposed. The Judge's stance is different in that, while he represents a dogmatic approach to Enlightenment thought, he himself is not enlightened. He may be a professional in terms of his position and legal training, and he may be educated, however he is neither enquiring nor curious. Rather, in the words of Wynne-Simmons, he is a character 'whose viewpoint was essentially a dead one' (ibid.). His is an unequivocal and despotic reason, one that cannot comprehend challenges to its world view. Instead the Judge is forced to acknowledge the evil phenomena using his adherence to empirical data. The Judge's intractability and stubbornness imply that his philosophical world – that of the urban, the modern, and the progressive – is flawed and potentially vulnerable to threats that its narrow ideology cannot comprehend or accommodate. The closedness of the Judge's reasoning stands in stark contrast to the apparent fluidity of the demon's influence that appears to gather supporters without any direct communion. Indeed, the Judge represents a troubled Enlightenment, and a paradox that was recognised within the philosophical movement even in the 18th century, certainly by Kant, who pondered 'what happens if men think without limits?' (Kant quoted in Outram, 2013: 2). If each and every man has the capacity to pursue reason and rationality entirely unfettered, then what will become of society? Kant reflected upon this and discerned a separation between 'public reason', whereupon each man is free to pursue reason without limit, and 'private reason', where his responsibilities of station and office limit his freedom to pursue reason. The Judge demonstrates this balance of public and private reason. His capacity for public reason supports his (ironically) clandestine support for the exiled Stuart monarchy, while his office as a Judge defines his 'private reason', as he has to upload the law and maintain the peace of the actual monarch, a monarch he does not believe should occupy the throne. And while he is happy to explore his capacity for reason, he expects others to fall in line with their social station – Ralph is reprimanded as a superstitious peasant, Peter lambasted as a foolish boy, Rosalind demeaned as an unsuitable bride.

This paradox of man's reason – that it must be constrained in case each man's unlimited freedom threaten the stability of society – was further explored by Horkheimer and Adorno in their *Dialectic of Enlightenment* (1947). From their perspective shortly after the devastation, total war, crimes against humanity and genocide perpetrated during the Second World War, the reason and rationality celebrated during the Enlightenment had not enhanced man's understanding of, and relationship with, the world, but had instead driven him further into barbarism and ignorance:

> The Enlightenment had always aimed at liberating men from fear and establishing their sovereignty. Yet the fully enlightened earth radiates disaster triumphant. The program of the Enlightenment was the disenchantment of the world: the disassociation of myths and the substitution of knowledge for fancy. (Horkheimer and Adorno, quoted in Outram, 2013: 5)

Horkheimer and Adorno saw the Second World War and the Holocaust as the ultimate and inevitable outcome of the homocentric, technological and rational aims of the Age of Reason. The very logistics of mechanised warfare and organised genocide – the mass displacement of populations to death camps, the mass movement of troops, the production of armaments, ammunition and gas – could not have been developed but for the pursuit of reason and the mastery of nature through rationality. The absolute devotion to man's unfettered capacity to understand nature through the prism of mathematical rationality, and through that comprehension to subordinate and control it, disassociated the world from 'superstition, mythology, fear, and revelation' (Outram, 2013: 6). In doing so, nature loses its esoteric authority, and the Enlightenment moves from a quest for knowledge to an exertion of authority over the natural world.

The Judge certainly represents this pessimistic vision of the Enlightenment. If the demon represents the resurgent wilderness then the Judge is the remorseless force of reason, who only attempts to understand nature in order to suppress it. The Judge's exhortation to extreme violence in order to defeat the demon can be read as illustrating the power of the demon and the lengths needed to oppose it, but it can also be read as the voice of unfettered reason. The total warfare of the world wars, achieved through the breakthroughs in strategy and technology that were built upon the foundations of Enlightenment reason and rationality, find a sinister parallel in the Judge's assertion that the innocent will be destroyed along with the guilty if it means the eradication of the demon.

The Judge, ever problematic, does not embody a solely pessimistic view of the Enlightenment. In contrast to Horkheimer and Adorno's bleak assessment of the rewards of Enlightenment thinking, the philosopher Jürgen Habermas has identified a far more optimistic outcome of the Age of Reason – that of the increased accessibility and value of knowledge. Habermas sees the Enlightenment as the point at which knowledge became commodified as information, and information was freely transacted. The 18th century, especially in Britain, was a time of public lectures, newspapers and periodicals, a time when the communication and consumption of information greatly accelerated. The Judge represents this point of view too. It is perhaps telling that the Judge is dismissive of the Doctor's superstitious tales but pays more attention when he sees the book of magic. As a printed tome, the Judge holds more store by it as it is a product of knowledge and a commodity of information recognisable to an urban man of reason in a way that oral folklore is not. The act of collating, writing and printing stories together substantiates the content in the Judge's eyes as a work of natural philosophy, which lack credibility as a series of disconnected spoken legends and customs. This is arguably the bourgeoisification and rationalisation of communal, immemorial knowledge, transformed via processes understood by the urban, propertied, educated class into trustworthy and reputable science.

The Jacobite Judge

It is even ambiguous as to whether the Judge represents the status quo at all. Towards the beginning of the film he makes a toast to His Catholic Majesty King James III, the son of the deposed James II of England and Ireland and VII of Scotland, much to Peter's discomfort. This act marks the Judge out as a Jacobite, a supporter of the exiled House of Stuart, rather than supporting the succession of James' daughters and son-in-law – William III (r. 1689-1702) & Mary II (r. 1689-1694), and Anne (r. 1702-

1714) – and the Hanoverian monarchs who succeeded them. The Judge, then, does not support or even represent the status quo, but instead covertly resists and opposes the established social and political hierarchy. As a Judge, he would have been required to make an oath of allegiance to the Anglican monarch, and one he would have done so out of political expediency rather than personal conviction. The former regimes of Charles II and, especially, James II were tainted by perceptions of autocracy and Papism. Roman Catholicism was considered to be enslaving, erroneous, corrupt and despotic, and thoroughly alien to Enlightened Britons in the 18th century who felt it was fundamentally tyrannical and irrational. The Judge is a member of the old guard, one associated with enslaving superstition and the tyranny of ignorance. He certainly demonstrates tyrannical traits when brow-beating Peter, Rosalind and Ralph, or when he favours and pushes for harsh measures of retaliation against the cult that will not distinguish the innocent from the guilty. Arguably, within the confines of these binary sets of characteristics, we would expect him to be far more credulous of the local folklore and more accommodating of their traditional rural customs and relationships. He is instead a thoroughly modern man, one more at home in his study surrounded by the new learning than he is receiving hospitality from the local Squire. Yet his affiliation for what would have been perceived as treasonous or redundant values stymies the effectiveness of his reason. Consequently the status quo is eroded and degraded further by the Judge's ostensible support for his values and his clandestine adherence to an inimical establishment.

THE SQUIRE

Squire Middleton is the local justice. Although originally a term that described a young apprentice to a knight during the Mediaeval period, by the late 17th and into the 18th centuries a Squire was a village leader, usually a member of the gentry, and typically the major landowner in the area who lived in the manor house. They were often related to peers, and could trace an illustrious lineage back to knights who had settled in the area many years ago. Frequently the Squire was also a Justice of the Peace or the local member of parliament.

The Squire in *Satan's Claw* is the principal source of authority in the village. In this role it is reasonable that we should expect to see him take an active stance in maintaining civil order and in containing the threat posed by the cult. Instead the Squire is absent for much of the central part of the film. He is involved very little in any action taken against the cult or indeed in any investigation into the murders of Mark and Cathy Vespers. While he becomes an active participant in the denouement, he is merely part of the mob of villagers and is not individualised with any specific or unique agency. In fact, his only active contribution to the narrative is to bring the force of the law to bear on the erroneous accusation made by Angel Blake against the Reverend Fallowfield.

While we could attribute this to the idiosyncratic structure of the film, when he does appear he is an impotent and flawed character who fails to exercise his duties effectively and as such leaves the village exposed to danger. He, like the Judge, is another signifier of the pessimistic and ambiguous narrative of the film. While the Squire is friendly and engaging, he demonstrates no capacity to manage order in the village. He tells the Judge of the villagers 'they love me, but they fear me first' but there is no evidence of this deferent obedience at all in the film. The very first scene in which we meet the Squire – where he is ordering troopers to continue the search for the missing Isobel Banham – his directives are met with a surreptitious muttering of 'silly old fool' by the soldiers. In fact, the Squire demonstrates inertia, disempowerment and poor judgement. He acts entirely on directions given to him by the Judge, demonstrating precious little autonomy, and the single occasion when he does act of his own accord his judgement and actions are misguided and based on a credulous acceptance of the duplicity of others. Not only does this undermine the Squire's ability to maintain the rule of law but it also allows for the further debilitation of authority in the village by legitimising an attack on another source of authority, the Curate.

The general incompetence and impotence of the Squire further exposes the flaws inherent in the systems and structures that he is both part of and that he represents, while also challenging any assumptions that the status quo is worth upholding and its values cherishing. It is understandable that, at the start of the film, Ralph takes his immediate concerns to the Banham house, as he works their lands. But it is telling that the Squire is not informed or consulted sooner, and this serves to diminish his agency further. Any agency of authority within the narrative is driven either by the Judge or, to a lesser extent, by Peter Edmonton, neither of whom are directly members of the village community. It is the Squire who forms the connection between the village and the outside world.

The Squire, then, is both a symptom, and an exemplar, of the paranoid narrative. His impotence and incompetence both contaminate, and become representative of, the status quo. It is interesting to compare this to the Judge's treasonous allegiances and doing so again illustrates how ambiguous and irresolute the narrative is. The Squire's inefficacy and flaws highlight the flaws and vulnerabilities inherent in the status quo. Given his key position within the status quo, both his deference to a superior who represents a clandestine and threatening alternative to that status quo, and his considerable disempowerment and lack of autonomy in comparison with the Judge, only further serves to degrade the value of the establishment and diminish its worth.

THE CURATE

Where Squire Middleton represents parochial secular authority, Reverend Fallowfield represents parochial religious authority. And, like the Squire, he is an impotent figure whose powerlessness illustrates the binary tension between order and disorder in the film.

Fallowfield's title tells us something about his position in the village, beyond merely being the community's priest. A curate was traditionally used as the title for priests who assisted the parish priest, rather than a title held by the parish priest himself. In the Church of England today, it is also used to refer to priests in their first post following their ordination. As such, the title has connotations of disempowerment either by virtue of subordination or inexperience.

The separation of Fallowfield from any active community leadership beyond Bible classes and presiding over Mark Vespers' funeral, his general lack of interaction with any of the adult villagers, serves to marginalise him within the community and diminishes his standing, rendering him an impotent figure. His arrest, imprisonment and torture at the hands of the Squire, all on the basis of Angel Blake's unsubstantiated accusations, again demonstrate his absence of authority and community standing, so quickly are the Squire and the villagers happy to accept his guilt. Even his name – Fallowfield – refers to the act of leaving a field uncultivated to allow for the soil to replenish its nutrients. As such it is suggestive of his lack of vitality and potency.

In common with Squire Middleton, Fallowfield's presence in the film is marked by his lack of agency, his inability to protect his flock or to guide and provide pastoral care. His efforts to instruct the village children in the Scripture are confounded by their easiness to distraction and disobedience. Aside from Cathy Vespers, the introduction of the claw to the class proves a simple challenge to their concentration on the Curate's lessons. Later, we see a second Bible class some days later and one attended by almost none of the village children; they have succumbed to the influence of Angel and the fiend. While the ease with which the village youth are lured to join the cult attests to the fiend's power, it also attests to Fallowfield's powerlessness and lack of influence. It is suggestive yet again that he has never carried any meaningful authority amongst his flock. None of the children have any difficulty in turning away from his teaching (again, aside from Cathy Vespers), nor does he make any particular efforts to win them back. His only success comes in resisting Angel's advances, when she appears in his office and attempts to seduce him. Although he resists temptation, his act of resistance is not presented as a victory or an act that empowers him. Instead it peculiarly acts to further disempower him, as it appears to take all his resolve even to master this small act of defiance.

As the marginalisation and disempowerment of the Squire disconnects the village from those wider networks of temporal authority, so the marginalisation of Fallowfield similarly disconnects the village from wider religious structures. Whereas the appearance of the Judge, even given his despotic and ambiguous character, provides some form of external secular authority, his clandestine adherence to the Catholic Old Pretender (and not to the lawful Anglican monarch) means that he cannot provide an analogous religious authority to compensate for the impotence of the Curate. The marginalisation and diminution of the Reverend Fallowfield is, of course, symptomatic of the wider absence of Christianity within the film.

We can also see him as an expression of a number of changes to religious attitudes during the Age of Reason. In 1689, as part of the Glorious Revolution, the Act of Toleration was passed, granting certain freedoms of worship to non-Conformist Protestant denominations. While a modern audience may not feel it was especially tolerant, by contemporary standards it was quite radical in recognising that dissenters had the right to certain freedoms of worship. At the same time, Britain's growing colonies and commercial activity opened up the populace to a far greater contact with other faiths and cultures beyond Europe. This increased pluralism, alongside the state's acknowledgment of the validity of other forms of worship (indeed, the outright celebration by Enlightened thinkers of this tolerance and emancipation of religious expression), and philosophies of the Enlightenment that stressed mankind's capacity to understand nature through reason rather than revelation, slowly undermined many of the key values that had maintained Christianity's pre-eminence for so long. Additionally those aspects of the Church that had strengthened its authority were diminished: it no longer had a monopoly over education (although what we see in *Satan's Claw* is church-led schooling), the reach of church courts was considerably curtailed, and from 1717 the Convocation (the government of the church) was prorogued for effectively more than a century (Porter, 2000: 98). Man's capacity for reason was evidence for God's capacity for reason, and vice-versa; consequently reason and rationality were applied to the Church and the more revelatory, ritualised and mystical aspects of worship and belief were de-emphasised in favour of a religion that was focused more on being socially useful.

The Curate is certainly no Enlightened thinker by this measure – his faith seems far more sensual and mystical. In his first scene Ralph and the Judge find him roaming the hedgerows and catching snakes. During their exchange when they ask him if he knows of any recent strange occurrences, he references the death of one Meg Parsons and notes that strange folk do pass through the village on occasion. It is telling that these are the first words spoken by Fallowfield in the film, and they are remarks about folk belief and local custom. His presence outside, rather than in his church also is suggestive of a commune with nature and something almost pagan.

THE DOCTOR

Where the Squire and the Curate represent local secular and religious authority, the unnamed Doctor represents received scientific and medical knowledge.

The 17th century is held to be when the Scientific Revolution took place in Western

Europe and describes a long period of time that marked the emergence of what we would describe as modern science, including the definition of modern chemistry, astronomy, biology, mathematics and physics. The development of empirical and rational modes of study fundamentally changed the relationship between mankind and the natural world, and emphasised man's ability to perceive, study, understand and (ultimately) master the world around him. The Scientific Revolution was the precursor to the Enlightenment, or Age of Reason, when scientific process and methods were applied to society, politics, philosophy and culture. As we have discussed, the Judge is a man firmly grounded in the rational age of Scientific Revolution and the Enlightenment. He represents the 'knowledgeable absolutism' – for want of a better phrase – of the 1700s that determined that, while all things were not understood, all things *could* be understood and, through understanding, be mastered by man.

From a modern perspective, the title 'doctor' is invariably associated with science. However, these are anachronistic concepts when considering the early 18th century. There was no separate, defined field of study known as science, and there were precious few organisations devoted to its study (the oldest in existence, The Royal Society – formerly The Royal Society of London for Improving Natural Knowledge – was established in 1660). 'Science' and 'scientist' were only coined as terms in the 1830s. Before then the nearest approximation was 'natural philosophy', since "'nature" was the very subject matter of science' (Outram, 2013: 100). The relationship between natural philosophy and theology was very close, the two being inextricably linked, given that the aim of natural philosophy was to understand the world created by God. Natural philosophy then was fundamentally connected with religion. The meaning of 'nature', though, was complex. It was used to describe and illustrate God's divine order and design. Nature was considered to have been established by God as a habitat for man, in which man could carry out God's purpose. In this way, the wilderness and the natural world had been designed for mankind's occupation and use. 'Nature' was also held to be a state of being, a form that was uncorrupted, objectively good and pure. As such, for Enlightenment thinkers, 'nature' was not only the topography of our world, but was a space that mankind had God-given dominion over, a space that represented divine design, and a space that represented absolute moral virtue (Outram, 2013: 101).

It is the Judge who is the natural philosopher in *Blood on Satan's Claw*. The Doctor does not represent this new learning; rather, he represents older professions and customs. His acquaintance with, and acceptance of, folk medicine and the supernatural as a cause for ailments associates him with the traditions of cunning folk and white witches. His diagnosing Isobel Banham and his administering of treatments are the practice of a physician, while his (albeit very reluctant) removal of the devil's fur from Margaret's thigh demonstrates that he has some surgical knowledge. Crucially, though, his administration of treatments and surgical procedures are still based in a decidedly pre-Enlightenment philosophy. In fact, the Doctor stubbornly refuses to embrace the reason espoused by the Judge.

'How do we know, sir, what is dead?' The Judge, the Doctor and interaction of old and new knowledge © *Tigon*

The Doctor represents a different form of knowledge, and one that will be marginalised and supplanted by the developments and definitions ushered in by the Scientific Revolution. Where the Judge has a dogmatic faith in the scientific and the rational, the Doctor's points of reference are to the arcane superstitions and folk beliefs that are the relics of pre-Christian antiquity. The first time we meet the Doctor – when he is treating Isobel Banham for the scratches she has received from Rosalind – he refers to his absence of knowledge, and the gaps in information left to him from antiquity; a very clear contrast to the Judge's absolute confidence in his knowledge. The Doctor functions as a way of allowing the fading, old, rural ways to comment upon the intrusion of the new, empirically-based, rational science being developed in the urban spaces. His reaction to the Judge's disbelief that witchcraft could still be alive and thriving in the village (something the rational Judge from the busy and modern city of London would find to be utterly alien to his understanding of the world) is to admonish him with 'you are of the city; you cannot know the ways of the country'. This neatly establishes two opposing forms of knowledge that, while attempting to understand the same universe, approach it with very different methods, values and practices.

The urban space's expansive urge to understand and rationalise that which does not fit into its frameworks of knowledge is inextricably linked to its urge to control. Through acts of rationalisation and demarcation, what was once unknown is subordinated to civilised authority. It is very telling though that in *Satan's Claw* the obscure knowledge that the Doctor does have in his tome on witchcraft can only be used by the Judge once he has assimilated the contents in London (and as such in the heartland of civilisation). In so doing, he effectively redefines it as part of the accumulated modern scientific corpus of knowledge. Once the Judge returns, witchcraft no longer 'belongs' to the rural, the ancient or the parochial. It is only by acknowledging witchcraft as a force equivalent to the new sciences of biology, chemistry and astronomy, that it can be defeated by civilisation.

The Judge and the Doctor therefore represent two conflicting sources of learning and a comprehension of the natural world. The old-world learning of the Doctor – with its blending of magic, mysticism and Classical traditions, and its focus on humours, elements, substances and hermetic notions of a spiritual universe – would be confronted and gradually replaced by the new Enlightened learning of the Judge that viewed nature as a mechanical structure, 'as matter in motion, governed by laws capable of mathematical expression' (Porter, 2000: 138). Reason rationalised the old forms of knowledge, those associated with magic, esotericism and the occult. Gradually, there were definitions as to what natural philosophy was, and the most reasonable and rational way of mapping and understanding nature: chemistry overtook alchemy, astronomy superseded astrology. The older traditions were classified instead as 'pseudo-sciences' and rejected as superstitious or mystical. What had once been esteemed and respected philosophies failed the test of reason and were relegated to the scorned fringes of civilisation: 'Ancient wisdom lost its legitimacy as a scientific posture muscled in' (Porter, 2000: 150). As such, the traditions that the Doctor has built his knowledge around are waning in the face of the forceful rationalisation of the Judge's reason, another example of the encroachment of civilisation further and further out from the urban centres and into the rural landscapes.

However, critically neither the Doctor nor the Judge separately has the capacity to prevent the resurrection of the devil. It requires the occult knowledge of the Doctor, mediated via the reason of the Enlightened Judge, to defeat it. The restoration of the power of the ancient wilderness can only be opposed by the interaction between old and new knowledge.

Anarchy in the UK

Sixties idealism to Seventies cynicism

Despite its period setting and cod antique dialogue, *The Blood on Satan's Claw* feels far more contemporary to Britain in the 1970s than Hammer's horrors with their Manichaean outlook and invariably morally upright and triumphant status quos. *Satan's Claw* shares a similar sense of pessimism, cynicism and anomie to several other films made at the tail end of the 60s and into the next decade, from the oft mentioned *Witchfinder General*, to Michael Reeves' previous film *The Sorcerers* (1967), *Death Line* (1972, dir. Gary Sherman), and even the generally lacklustre *Cry of the Banshee* (1970, dir. Gordon Hessler), as well as to Pete Walker's downbeat films later that decade.

Certainly *The Blood on Satan's Claw* was very consciously born from the failure of the ideals of the sixties youth movements and a growing sense of disenchantment amongst the young, and this was clear to Wynne-Simmons and Haggard, both of whom were part of this counter-culture generation. There is a sense in the film both that the younger generation have failed, but also that they have been failed. 'Britain in the 1970s was a frightened and frightening place' (Easterbrook, 2013), the high optimism of the mid-sixties very starkly giving way to profound anxieties about the state of society, as well as continuous political and economic crises. The decade saw the country beset by strikes, industrial malaise, states of emergency, rampant inflation and seemingly endless strike action:

> Strikes, which had for some years been dominated by wildcat stoppages … became ever larger, ever more disruptive during Heath's time as prime minister. In 1970 the number of working days lost in industrial action was 11 million, the highest total since 1926, the year of the General Strike. (Turner, 2013: 11)

Industrial action, the sort that had the capability to bring essential services to a standstill both frequently and often, formed a backdrop of bubbling unrest from the mid-sixties and into the seventies. There was a pronounced fear, shared by many, about the sustainability of society and culture – the basic elements of fuel, food, heat and light:

> The autumn of 1970 saw the first real slide into chaos with the so-called dirty jobs strike by local council workers in London. Refuse collectors seeking higher wages

were joined by workers at refuse dumps ... and by sewerage workers. By mid-October more than 60,000 workers were on strike. (Turner, 2013: 10)

This industrial action led to the closure of schools and parks, environmental damage as untreated sewage was pumped into British rivers, and public health hazards as vast mountains of rubbish was left to accumulate in parts of London. These strikes may have occurred after the filming for *The Blood on Satan's Claw* was completed, but its production took place against a background of socio-political disharmony in the UK that culminated in this quasi-apocalyptic scenario, one that would be revisited throughout the seventies.

Beyond labour crises, the tide was turning on a series of social trends and legislative reforms of the sixties. The Labour government under Harold Wilson in the second half of that decade undertook a significant programme of social reform that has since been characterised as a 'sexual revolution' and one that accompanied a general tide of liberalisation across British society and culture. Abortion was legalised in 1967, the same year that the Family Planning Act made contraception readily available via NHS local health authorities, and that the Sexual Offences Act decriminalised homosexual acts in private between consenting adult men. Two years later, the Divorce Reform Act removed the emphasis on fault from divorce petitions and permitted the dissolution of marriage on the grounds of irretrievable breakdown. In 1968 the Lord Chancellor's powers of censorship over the theatre ceased, while there was a general trend towards a greater degree of explicit language and content in films passed by the BBFC, and a creeping increase in the visibility of pornographic material, as the decade wore on. While the impact of these reforms and trends can be overstated, undeniably they set the tone for what the status quo would permit and society would accommodate, and gave many the encouragement to begin to embrace in public what was previously regarded as shameful, unspoken or private. The perception of many, though, was that this new legislation gave license to the younger generation to indulge in all manner of wayward, offensive and self-harming behaviours, ones that were threatening to society at large:

Teenage promiscuity is a central part of the legend of the Swinging Sixties. Brian Masters [the British biographer], for example, claims that teenagers in the sixties were 'the first generation since the war to decide that the mysteries of sex should be explored and discoveries made for the sheer fun of it. People copulated on the slightest pretext after an acquaintance of some minutes.' (Sandbrook, 2007: 489)

The Wilson government's legislating for new or wider freedoms in the spheres of sexuality and marriage, coupled with other social reforms such as the temporary suspension and then permanent abolition of the death penalty for murder in Great Britain and the wider permissive trends in society and culture, crystallised for many into a perception that moral decay would inevitably lead to an increase in criminal behaviour, an erosion in Christian values, and a decline in public order, fundamentally degrading the state at large:

[the link between moral permissiveness and violent crime] was not necessarily a fanciful connection, for censorship had indeed been relaxed and there was no doubt that crime had recently increased. In 1955 there had been fewer than 6000 violent crimes against the person, but by 1960 there were more than 11,000, and by 1969 more than 21,000. (Sandbrook, 2007: 571)

While we should be cautious in drawing any direct causative link, many certainly felt that there was a relationship between perceived moral laxity and the tribulations of Britain in terms of rising crime and industrial unrest. The new Conservative government under Edward Heath spearheaded a backlash against both perceived moral laxity and the erosion of respect and order, 'if the "permissive" 1960s were made possible by a proliferation of liberalising legal reforms, the early 1970s witnessed a counter-strike of punitive legislation' (Hunt, 1998: 17).

The government was not alone in seeking to stymie the increased liberal trajectory in society and culture and the perceived association with the corrosion of public order and virtue. Figures such as the former Labour cabinet minister Lord Longford, founder of the National Viewers' and Listeners' Association (NVLA) Mary Whitehouse, satirist Malcolm Muggeridge, and pop star Cliff Richard, all made public stands against various aspects of what they perceived as the permissive society and promoted a restoration of vanishing moral values. Longford established his own enquiry into tackling the problem of pornography, the committee including both Richard and Muggeridge (Turner, 2008: 141-142), while Mary Whitehouse became a household name through her attempts to restore Christian values to British society, founding the Clean Up TV Campaign in 1964 and the NVLA in 1965 (Sandbrook, 2007: 577-578). Even the novelist Dennis Wheatley, a man much acquainted with the popularity of alternative lifestyles and ways of thinking, was condemnatory of the permissive generation and its celebration of excessive behaviours:

> Dennis Wheatley had a stern warning for the love generation: human behaviour, he said, has entered a new phase. It is termed the permissive society. The restraining powers of the church, parental authority, and public opinion have been overthrown by the younger generation. (Sweet, 2015)

Whitehouse, Longford and Muggeridge were instrumental in the founding of The Festival of Light, a grass-roots Christian movement that aimed to restore Christian morals to the nation and that held a series of nationwide rallies in 1971 against permissiveness. In this context we may view the Judge in *The Blood on Satan's Claw* as much a moral crusader of the late sixties and seventies, as a man of the 18th century Enlightenment. His repressive bullying of Peter, his censuring against dangerous women, and his ruthlessness in suppressing the cult and its activities (even to the point of slaughtering the innocent with the guilty, as some of the villagers fear) mark him out as a similar to the more extreme aspects, and tyrannical caricatures, of Whitehouse, Longford and Muggeridge. Whitehouse has been quoted as saying 'freedom dies when moral anarchy takes over. It lives when citizens accept limitations upon themselves for the greater good of the community as a whole' (quoted in Turner, 2008: 133), a sentiment that is easy to imagine being expressed by the Judge in the Banham's parlour.

Written, shot and produced as it was over 1970, *The Blood on Satan's Claw* sits on the cusp of the decline of 1960s hippy counter-cultural hedonism and the rise in the anti-permissive moral backlash. As such it is perhaps unsurprising that the film both critiques the repressiveness of the status quo, and the danger inherent in counter-cultural ideas and behaviours. The cult in the film is a loose agglomeration of traits and elements perceived to be part of the hippy counter-culture: the cultists are mostly teenagers; they are marked as social drop-outs by virtue of their removal from the established social space of the village and their re-location to the forest as a quasi-commune, a move that also implicitly identifies them as close to nature ('flower power'); they are bedecked with floral garlands, and wear loose white robes; they demonstrate a free attitude to nudity and indulge in transgressive sexual activities; they appear to worship nature and carry out pagan-inflected rituals; and at the end of the film they appear to take part in what many viewers would have identified as a drug fuelled happening. However, the reactionary fear of the disorder that results from immorality is present in the film too in the brutality that appears inevitable when youth are isolated from the status quo and vulnerable to corrupting influences. The film plays both sides out to their extreme conclusions, offering a bleak commentary to what was going on in the real world, with the youth revolution collapsing into violence, corrupted innocence and demoralisation, and the establishment backlash waiting in the wings to re-impose order and virtue with authoritarian relish. The overt violence, sexual assault and nudity of *Satan's Claw* also suggest a repressed fascination for the prurient, as if the film were the gaze of the shocked, reactionary status quo, both horrified and titillated by what they see.

Corrupted innocence – the twilight of the youth revolution © Tigon

This fear that the young generation had become corrupted is visible throughout the film. Mark Morris terms this fear 'ephebiphobia' – a fear of youth (Haggard, 2019, sleeve notes by Morris). The hippy counter-culture of the sixties was the latest in a number of youth-orientated movements that had gained expression in post-war Britain, influenced by American culture, such as the Teddy Boys and the Mods and the Rockers, as well as a steady increase in hooliganism amongst young British football fans from the 1960s onwards. These movements were associated with rebellion and violence and were the subject of concern on the part of the Establishment and the media. The Easter weekend of 1964 saw the violent clash of rival gangs of teenagers on Clacton seafront, with the nation's leading newspaper *The Mirror* reporting the following day:

The Wild Ones invaded a seaside town yesterday – 1,000 fighting, drinking, roaring, rampaging teenagers on scooters and motorcycles … [they] attacked people in the streets, turned over parked cars, broke into beach huts, smashed windows and fought with rival gangs. (Quoted in Sandbrook, 2007: 203)

It was the prelude to a number of sporadic pitched battles between gangs of Mods and Rockers that interrupted the usual tranquillity of several British coastal resorts across 1964 including at Margate, Brighton and Bournemouth, resulting in hundreds of arrests and thousands of pounds worth of criminal damage. Prior to the Mods and Rockers, the Teddy Boys had caused consternation amongst the media and middle-class of Britain of the 1950s, becoming a shorthand for delinquent and threatening youth. The Hammer horror/science-fiction hybrid *The Damned* (US title, *These are the Damned*, 1961, dir. Joseph Losey), based on H. L. Lawrence's novel *The Children of Light* (1960), features an aggressive, anti-social gang of Teddy Boys-cum-bikers in a British coastal town. While the plot of the book and the film is not concerned with gang violence, they were clearly considered so much part of the perception of the cultural demography of the British seaside that their inclusion almost seemed inevitable. As the sixties moved into the seventies a new youth culture fermented, that of the skinhead:

… by 1972 it was being argued that they 'constitute by far the biggest single group amongst the country's teenagers'. And their image was one of mindless violence aimed at rival gangs, especially in football grounds, and at ethnic minorities. (Turner, 2013: 63)

The character and activities of these youth groups were exaggerated by press coverage that was as given to sensation as it was reportage. While many newspapers that covered the 'battle' of the Mods and Rockers on Clacton seafront were determined to do so in the most lurid and inflammatory terms – *The Telegraph,* for example, calling them 'grubby hordes of louts and sluts' (quoted in Sandbrook, 2007: 208) – a significant minority were far more moderate in their coverage. *The New Statesman,* for example, stated that 'there was no evidence of drink or drugs and no gang warfare' (ibid.), whilst others, like *The Times,* drew attention to the fact that these supposed gang members were from middle-class households and not some dangerous, disenfranchised underclass (Sandbrook, 2007: 209). Similarly, the earlier youth figure of the Teddy Boy was subject to salacious sensationalism on the part of the British media, while the exploits of skinheads sensationalised in the *Skinhead* novels of Richard Allen (1970-1980) that followed the life of fictional 16-year old Joe Hawkins 'a member of a thuggish skinhead gang whose life revolved around drinking, sex, and beating people up' (Brotherstone and Lawrence, 2017: 559). However, the facts of the behaviour of youth gangs and movements are almost beside the point; crucially there was an audience – predominantly a middle-class one – that bought into this perception of these youth cultures as dangerous and corrupting. The act of young people forming into gangs and groupings independently of adult direction and control was a source of anxiety. These groups became totemic of the vulnerability of youth, not only to pernicious, anti-social influences but also as a route by which these influences might insidiously make its way into the middle-class, bourgeois home and the heart of the status quo. *The Blood on Satan's Claw* is clearly influenced by these pervasive fears about the organisation of teenagers into youth gangs that sit outside adult control, but also by concerns that these youth movements are fundamentally inimical to the values, structures and vitality of the status quo.

Beyond these broad cultural trends and a zeitgeist of social anxieties, there were two specific and significant real-life instances of youthful corruption and the failure of sixties ideals that had a profound effect on Wynne-Simmons and Haggard and their shaping of *Satan's Claw*, with both explicitly citing them in interviews as especially formative in terms of scripting and production: the Tate-LaBianca Murders committed by members of the Charles Manson Family, and the case of British child murderer Mary Bell.

THE MANSON FAMILY

Between 8-10 August 1969, seven people were murdered in Los Angeles by members of the Charles Manson 'Family'. Under the direction of Charles Manson, three of his Family – Tex Watson, Susan Atkins and Patricia Krenwinkel – entered the home of film director Roman Polanski and killed the occupants, including Polanski's eight-month pregnant wife Sharon Tate (Polanski was in London at the time). The following night, again under the direction of Manson, Tex Watson, Patricia Krenwinkel and another

Family member Leslie Van Houten, killed Leno and Rosemary LaBianca at their home (according to the accounts of the killers, Manson had already entered the house and tied up the victims). These murders have since become known as the Tate-LaBianca Murders and, for many contemporary and later commentators, were the death knell of the so-called Summer of Love.

The murders were notorious across the globe for several reasons, aside from the celebrity status of actress Sharon Tate and her association with Polanski. The killings themselves were extremely savage – 169 stab wounds and seven gun-shot wounds, an orgy of brutality (Watson, 2009). The killings appeared, at least initially, to be random with no evident motive for such violence. The murders also took place within the homes of the victims, a frightening attack on the idea of the home as a place of safety and security. The murder scenes too featured unnerving messages left by the killers, with 'pig' and 'healter [sic] skelter' daubed on the walls in the victims' blood, apparently following Manson's command to his Family to leave something 'witchy' at the scene. The murders therefore seemed to say that no one could be safe, not even in your own home, from a seemingly senseless, extremely horrifying, and almost occultishly graphic assault.

Perhaps the most repulsive, yet attractive, aspect of the whole crime was Manson himself, and the Family he had created. Vincent Bugliosi, the chief prosecutor in the sensational trial that followed (the longest in US history at that point, and one that would have been starting as production on *Satan's Claw* was concluding), is clear in the reasoning behind why the Manson Family terrified the public: 'The other thing that terrified the nation so much is when the identity of the killers became known. And who were they? Young kids from average American homes with fairly good backgrounds. There was a feeling that this could be our own children' (Bugliosi quoted in Watson, 2009). Many members of the Family, including Atkins and Krenwinkel, were from middle-class and apparently respectable families, not the stereotypically poor or troubled backgrounds usually considered to be the breeding ground for crime. But their comfortable backgrounds obscured a myriad of causal factors – loneliness, isolation, addiction, depression, low self-worth – that led many of them to the Family. The Family was a commune of around 100 followers, mostly young women, which focused on hallucinogenic drug use, free-love, and a messianic devotion to Charles Manson himself.

THE BLOOD ON SATAN'S CLAW

The notion that these communes, once the province of hippies and their ideals of peace of love, could become corrupted, was a key influence on Robert Wynne-Simmons:

> ... the cults were not all purity and innocence. Michele Dotrice's character – her devotion against all the odds to what was happening – and the power that Linda Hayden's character held, has something to do with the really weird devotion that Manson's followers had to him. (Wynne-Simmons in Taylor, 1996)

There are a number of similarities in the folk culture of both the Manson Family and the demonic cult in *Satan's Claw* that illustrate the influence of Manson's real-world Family on Angel Blake's fictional one. Although we tend not to see Angel and her followers recruit new members (rather, the new additions we see are almost immediately sacrificed), the luring of victims Mark and Cathy does bear the hallmarks of introduction into the group. Manson would test potential new recruits by watching their reactions to the Family's sexual orgies or by asking them if they would die for him (Fine, 1982: 49); we can see parallels with what happens to Cathy in particular, who becomes the centrepiece in a horrifying sexual ritual before having to offer herself up for the demon's resurrection through her sacrifice. There are parallels with Ralph too at the end of the film, where he is clearly bewitched by the erotically inflected ritual to the point of destroying himself by offering up his leg to complete the corporeality of the demon. Similarly, both the Family and the cult, in common with the folk culture of other small, cultic groups, establish boundaries between themselves and others through lore that is specific and limited to members only. The lore is particular to the group because their understanding of it gives them a unique insight that marks them out as special and separate to the rest of society. Where the Manson Family drew in a large array of cultural knowledge, from the Bible to the Beatles to Masonic Lore and science fiction, as well as prison folklore (Fine, 1982: 50), the cult have the book of Behemoth that Margaret reads from, as well as ritualised rape and mutilation, that are distinct to them and a unique source of meaning and insight to members. The folklore of the group also functions to keep the group separate from society at large (especially if the group sees itself in opposition to society), to reaffirm their sense of specialness, and to have a meaningful function in binding the group together. For the Manson Family much of their folklore lay in rituals and behaviours designed to offend social sensibilities and to normalise that offensive behaviour, from handling live rattlesnakes to simulating snuff films and other bizarre sexual activity (Fine, 1982: 52). The cult of *Satan's Claw* is similarly bound by behaviour that offends social values – murder, rape, disfigurement – as well as rituals that unite the group, such as the May blossom procession prior to Cathy's ritualised murder. The folk culture of both groups also asserts and reinforces their social hierarchies. The ritual and lore of the Family elevated Manson to the role of messianic leader and asserted his place at the top. Miracles and myths were attributed to Manson, attesting to his almost supernatural abilities. The Family acted out an imitation of the Crucifixion with Manson as Jesus Christ, hoisting him aloft on a cross while Family members played out the roles of apostles and accusers (ibid.). Similarly, the cult celebrates and reinforces Angel's leadership role – she appears to preside over the rituals and other members defer to her through behaviour or expression. When Margaret finds herself at the Vespers' cottage and attempts to return to the cult, her overriding fear is rejection by Angel, which is the same as expulsion from the cult and a loss of specialness and unique insight. The folk culture of groups like these frequently imposed severe punishments for member's disclosing even apparently trivial knowledge to outside parties, something that Margaret is aware, and terrified, of. As feared, Angel does punish Margaret through expulsion and in leaving her to be mauled by the Judge's dogs.

The Tate-LaBianca murders also have parallels to the killings and rituals in *Satan's Claw*. In both cases, the domestic space is exposed as fundamentally unsafe, with extremely graphic violence taking place there (whether frenzied stabbings and shootings or the hysterical self-amputation of hands). Manson's order to the murderers to leave something 'witchy' at the scene – an expression of a folkloric mish-mash of pop culture Satanism, counter-culture, paganism and hippyism that swirled around the Family – is equally as pervasive if similarly nebulous in *Satan's Claw*.

This anxiety about the indoctrination of the young by pernicious influences and people remains a deeply held societal fear playing on the commonly held beliefs in the innocence of youth and its vulnerability to corruption through the passive, uncritical acceptance of extreme ideas. It has arisen again recently both in the worry about the so-called Islamic State brainwashing children to fight for them, and even in the supposed manipulation of climate change activist Greta Thunberg by abusive adults. Curiously in *Satan's Claw*, abuse by elders is not the focus of the youth cult. While the cult is influenced by the demon, it is explicitly led by Angel, another child. Where we do witness abuse by elders is in the Banham house, when Rosalind and Peter are both physically assaulted by the Judge and Isobel. While the occasions are ostensibly to control Rosalind's screaming and Peter's upset, both actions are so extreme in the face of reasoning behind them (Isobel hitting Rosalind to quieten her, and the Judge striking Peter to calm him) that they can only be interpreted as an opportunity by the elders to suborn the young people to them and to act out their condemnation of Peter and Rosalind's relationship. Given either the disembodiment or general absence of the demon for much of the film, Angel is the real leader of the cult, which means that *Satan's Claw* sees the manipulation and corruption of children by another child. This illustrates the other major real-life influence on the film: the child murderer Mary Bell.

MARY BELL

In 1968, 11-year old Mary Bell was found guilty of manslaughter, on the grounds of diminished responsibility, for the deaths of two toddlers in Newcastle-upon-Tyne – four-year old Martin Brown and three-year old Brian Howe. In both cases the children had been found strangled, and, in the case of Brian Howe, his body had signs of mutilation (the police reports of the time concluded that Bell had returned to the scene of her second crime to carve an 'M' into the boy's stomach and mutilate his genitals). Another girl, Norma Bell, a friend (but no relation) of Mary's was tried alongside her as she had been present during the killing of Brian Howe but was acquitted. The case horrified the public and even the press, usually keen to capitalise on the sensational aspects of notorious murder cases, were relatively subdued in their reporting. The BBC, to avoid disturbing younger members of their audience, deliberately did not cover it during the 6 o'clock news, and the press galleries in court were only full for the first, the sixth (the date of Mary's cross-examination) and the final two days of the trial. It was as if the crime – that of children killing children – was so shocking that there was an unspoken covenant across media and public alike that it needed to be contained. If the crime itself was not shocking enough, then Mary's behaviour after the murders and during the trial was even more disquieting. Four days after the death of Martin Brown, Mary knocked on the door of the Browns' house, smiling and asking to play with him. June Brown,

Martin's mother recounted: 'I said, "No pet, Martin is dead". She turned round and said, "Oh, I know he's dead. I wanted to see him in his coffin," and she was still grinning' (Brown quoted in Sereny, 1995: 27). Chief Inspector Dobson, the officer who led on the case, recalled seeing Mary when Brian Howe's coffin was brought out of his family home on the day of his funeral: 'She stood there, laughing. Laughing and rubbing her hands' (Sereny, 1995: 50).

The concept of murderous children was not a new one in cinema by 1970, and the coming decade would see a proliferation of homicidal children and deadly babies (*The Omen*, 1976, dir. Richard Donner; *The Exorcist; I Don't Want to be Born*, 1975, dir. Peter Sasdy; *Damien: Omen II*, 1978, dir. Don Taylor). However, the majority of these films featured violence perpetrated upon adults by malevolent youngsters, not violence inflicted by children on each other. The overwhelming uneasiness of the case of Mary Bell was the sense of children deliberately brutalising each other, something that clearly affected and influenced Robert Wynne-Simmons:

> ... she would go up to the mothers of the children she'd murdered and virtually boast of it. She seemed to want to get herself caught and that idea of childhood innocence being totally evil was also a central theme of the movie. (Wynne-Simmons quoted in Taylor, 1996: 88)

The case of Mary Bell threw an uncomfortable spotlight onto childhood innocence and questioned its integrity, something the public at large found disturbing to face, just as the tragic murder of James Bulger would do 25 years later. The public, the media, and even those professionals involved in cases like this – from police to psychologists – often fell back on the notion of the bad seed, an idea frequently explored as the rationale behind most of the deadly children of seventies horror cinema – they were *born* bad. The general impression of Mary was that she was evil and born wicked – 'what we have here was *not* a "sick" child, but a clever little MONSTER' (Sereny, 1995: 80; all emphases as in original text) – and the press described her as a 'bad seed', 'evil birth' and 'child monster'. Simple labels such as these do not attempt to understand the reasoning behind Mary's killing of other children, but instead attempt to safely contain the threat. Far more reassuring to the public at large to ascribe Mary's aberrant and abhorrent behaviour to her simply being born bad, rather than to consider the complex familial, social and other circumstances that may have nurtured and permitted these behaviours.

Mary's behaviour and attitudes during the investigation and trial have had a clear influence on *Blood on Satan's Claw*. Mary was described by many of those who spent any length of time with her as manipulative of, and indifferent to, the feelings of those around her. Dr David Westbury, the Home Office Forensic Psychiatrist who examined Mary, said 'To Mary ... manipulation of people is the primary aim – it is much more important to her than what she actually achieves with it' (Westbury quoted in Sereny, 1995: 65). A policewoman who had responsibility for Mary during her trial stated that 'she had no feelings for other people' (Sereny, 1995: 83). The behaviour of Mary Bell is a clear influence on Angel Blake, who is similarly manipulative, particularly evident in her accusation of sexual assault levelled at Reverend Fallowfield. Her youth and apparent innocence is not questioned by her father and the Squire, who immediately accost the Curate. She is also manipulative in convincing others to do her bidding; Margaret is especially in the thrall of Angel and she is distraught when Angel leaves her to be hunted down by the Judge's hounds. Mary was described by many as having a magnetic personality, particularly controlling and manipulative of her friend Norma. Mr Lyons, the prosecuting counsel, in his summing up said:

> ... eleven-year old Mary had wielded over thirteen-year old Norma 'an evil and compelling influence almost like that of the fictional Svengali' and later 'In Mary you have a most abnormal child, aggressive, vicious, cruel, incapable of remorse, a girl moreover possessed of a dominating personality, with a somewhat unusual intelligence and a degree of cunning that is almost terrifying'. (Lyons quoted from Sereny, 1995: 166).

The arrogant glee that Mary appeared to take in flaunting her knowledge of the murders in front of the victims' families finds form outside of Angel Blake – the behaviour of the youth who emerges from the woodland to harass Ellen Vespers and smash the bottle of medicine she had for Mark is very similar, him goading and laughing that they have put Mark in the woodshed.

The infamous crimes of killers like Mary Bell and the Manson Family are mediated through *The Blood on Satan's Claw* as a commentary on civilisation. Their actions – the wilful destruction of individuals within their families, communities and neighbourhoods, as well as the ferocity and callousness of their violence – demonstrate that the isolation and insularity supposed to be the lot of the rural is not limited to rural localities, and that this notion of the pernicious and dangerous 'local' can be found anywhere. The regressive, inwardly focused horror of these hermetic communities, families and individuals demonstrate the failure of civilisation; points of stagnation where civilised values have eroded, progress has faltered and society appears to regress and feed upon itself. In the case of *Satan's Claw*, the locality is quite literally feeding upon itself, destroying itself to recreate a threat that has emerged from beneath their feet.

A CRISIS IN ENGLISH IDENTITY

When *The Blood on Satan's Claw* was released in 1971, its concerns with the sudden re-emergence of our esoteric, pre-civilised past were especially topical:

> There was a pendulum swing away from the 1950s and the 1940s and the visions of rationality and technology and progress, and what's at the end of that is the mystic, the pagan, the occult. (Kim Newman quoted in Sweet, 2015)

The late sixties and early seventies saw renewed interest in the occult and the esoteric in Britain. Such tendencies can perhaps be traced back further, to the release of *Night of the Demon* (1957, dir. Jacques Tourneur) – based on MR James' short story 'Casting the Runes' (1911) and Nigel Kneale's television serial *Quatermass and the Pit* (1958-1959, dir. Rudolph Cartier). Arguably though, the loosening of decorum and increased visibility of alternative youth-oriented lifestyles from the mid-sixties onwards gave greater licence to the exploration of the mystical and profane.

This renewed fascination for the occult intersected with another cultural renaissance, a revival interest in British folk history. In particular, British television saw a flowering of series and serials exploring the mystical, occult, folkloric and pagan heritage of Britain. *The Owl Service* (1969-70, dir. Peter Plummer, based on Alan Garner's 1967 novel), *Arthur of the Britons* (1972-73) and *Children of the Stones* are children's dramas focused on Britain's folkloric, historical past, and the occult inflections of the ancient pagan landscape. The Play for Today series visited the subject several times, in *Robin Redbreast* (1970, dir. James MacTaggart), *Penda's Fen, and Red Shift* (1978, dir. John Mackenzie, and based on Alan Garner's 1973 novel). Even the long running sci-fi series *Doctor Who* got in on the act in *The Daemons* (1971, dir. Christopher Barry), with a story about a powerful and ancient alien slumbering in an Anglo-Saxon barrow resurrected by what appears to be occult ritual and, later, *The Stones of Blood* (1978, dir. Darrol Blake) in which an alien criminal masquerades as a Celtic goddess overseeing megalithic monsters hidden within a stone circle.

Similarly, on film there was a pre-occupation with both the pagan heritage of Britain, and with telling the story of British folk, rather than that of the ruling classes. *Witchfinder General* and *The Wicker Man* focus on the lot of small rural British communities and their interactions with occult and pagan belief. Released the same year as *Satan's Claw* and a naked attempt to cash in on the success of *Witchfinder*, *Cry of the Banshee* also addresses the notion of a long established though clandestine coven of witches in Tudor England. Like many of these other examples of the revival of a fascination for pre-Christian Britain in British television and cinema, *The Blood on Satan's Claw* 'juxtaposes pagan vitality against the puritanical forces of order' (Cooper, 2011: 90).

The notion of Britain as an 'old country' (Wright, 1985, quoted in Monk and Sargeant (eds), 2002: 1) is one that is fundamental to the British national sense of self. British nationality is tied into the land of the British Isles as a discrete set of islands, and ones that are very, very old, with traces of that antiquity still visible and tangible, 'a nation whose identity resides crucially in the narratives, myths, landscapes and material and cultural artifacts of its past' (Monk and Sargent (eds), 2002: 1). These myths are inextricably tied up with our ancient landscapes and are usually deployed to form narratives to challenge conventional and accepted histories. Of particular interest in politically coding our antiquity in this way, is that our pagan past existed before the arrival of terms that we use to define Britain and British nationality; notions of 'British', 'English' or 'Christian' are much later constructs. Our pagan past then, appears to us to survive from a much more fluid and malleable age, something that can be both liberating and frightening as it 'appeals to neo-pagans and some counter-cultures as a means of rejecting and challenging the implications of what is often considered to be the repressive nature of Christian-based authority' (Krzywinska, 2017).

Much of this mythic history has been informed by the chronicles of Roman writers

Tactius and Caesar, and it is from their accounts that the perennial fascination between paganism and human sacrifice and black magic stems, informing accounts of druidic worship from 17th- and 18th-century antiquarians, such as William Stukeley and Reverend William Borlase, to the works of Dennis Wheatley (Soar, 2019: 11-12). This association is full bodied in *Satan's Claw*, where transgressive sexual violation and murder are ritually conducted with sacred ruins and within the sacred wilderness.

Underpinning these tensions between culture and counter-culture, permissive and repressive, and younger and older, was a concern that Britain had lost its way. For the older generation of the Establishment, the younger counter-cultural generation threatened to change and sweep away all that Britain was. For the younger generation though, the status quo itself represented a Britain that had lost its way through ossification and needed to be cleared away. The essence of what Britain meant, and what it meant to be British, became a subject addressed across a number of films and TV programmes of the 1960s and 1970s, sometimes obliquely, sometimes overtly. The heritage of Britain – mediated through its history and geography – was appropriated to represent or symbolise nationhood. The landscape of Britain 'became, and still is, the most important landscape in the national environmental ideology' (Short, 1991: 75) because it was here that 'traces of the old, weird Britain can still be unearthed' (Young, 2010: 16). *The Blood on Satan's Claw* is, at first glance, part of this loose grouping of media that explores the tensions between culture and counter-culture through the prism of occult paganism against a puritanical status quo. However, and unusually for the time it was made, the film stalls from pledging its allegiance to one particular side. The Judge and the cult presided over by Angel are both unsympathetic and dangerous with both having the capacity and will to cause harm. The film chooses to take both culture and counter-culture to their extremes, both destructive and ruthless forces, and suggests that their opposition leaves the future state of affairs ambiguous.

BIBLIOGRAPHY

Anderson, G-N (2019) 'The old ways', *Fortean Times* issue 381, David Sutton (ed.).

Anon, https://www.audible.co.uk/pd/Blood-on-Satans-Claw-Audiobook/B078J7CNCQ (accessed 24 April 2019).

Anon, https://bbfc.co.uk/education-resources/student-guide/bbfc-history/1960s (accessed 21 February 2020).

Anon, https://pro.imdb.com/name/nm0943859/about (accessed 16 August 2019).

Anon, https://www.imdb.com/title/tt0066849/releaseinfo?ref_=tt_ql_dt_2 (accessed 16 August 2019).

Anon, https://www.imdb.com/title/tt0066849/locations?ref_=tt_ql_dt_5 (accessed 20 October 2019).

Anon, https://sites.google.com/site/derelictionintheshires/other-sites/st-james-church-bix-brand (accessed 20 October 2019).

Anon, 'Historic population of Birmingham' *Birmingham City Council*, https://www.birmingham.gov.uk/cs/Satellite?c=Page&childpagename=Lib-Central-Archives-and-Herita ge%252FPageLayout&cid=1223092760414&pagename=BCC%252FCommon%252FWr apper%252FWrapper (accessed 6 November 2010).

Anon, 'Birmingham MB/CB: Historical statistics – Population'. *A Vision of Britain through Time. University of Portsmouth.* 2009, https://www.visionofbritain.org.uk/data_cube_ page.jsp?data_theme=T_POP&data_cube=N_TOT_POP&u_id=10101001&c_ id=10001043&add=N (accessed 6 November 2010).

Anon, 'Birmingham' *Office for National Statistics*, https://www.ons.gov.uk/ census/2011census (accessed 6 November 2010).

Anon, https://www.theguardian.com/commentisfree/2019/mar/11/shamima-begum-cult-victim-isis (accessed 20 September 2019).

Anon, https://metro.co.uk/2019/04/25/greta-thunberg-ignorant-brainwashed-child-abused-adults-says-corbyns-brother-9315481/ (accessed 20 September 2019).

Arya, R and Chare, N (2016) *Abject visions: powers of horror in art and visual culture*, Manchester: Manchester University Press.

BBFC (2019), personal correspondence with the author.

Brotherstone, S and Lawrence, D (2017), *Scarred for life, growing up in the dark side of the decade: Volume one, the 1970s*, Lonely Water Books.

Cooper, I (2011) *Witchfinder General*, Leighton Buzzard: Auteur.

Cooper, I (2016) *Frightmares: A history of British horror cinema*, Leighton Buzzard: Auteur.

Chibnall, S (2002) *Pete Walker and Gothic revisionism*, in *British Horror Cinema* (eds Chibnall, Steve and Petley, Julian), London: Routledge.

Creed, B (2007, sixth edition) *The monstrous feminine: film, feminism, psychoanalysis*, London: Routledge.

Dixon, W W (2017) *The Films of Terence Fisher: Hammer horror and beyond*, Leighton Buzzard: Auteur.

Easterbrook, A (2013) sleeve notes for *A Warning to the Curious*, Ghost Stories for Christmas DVD set, BFI DVD.

Fine, G A (1982) *The Manson family: The folklore traditions of a small group*, Journal of the Folkore Institute.

Freud, S (2003) *The Uncanny*, translated by David McLintock, London: Penguin.

Haggard, P (2016), personal correspondence with the author.

Haggard, P (2019) *The Blood on Satan's Claw* [Blu Ray], Screenbound Pictures Ltd:

'Underneath Satan's Skin': New interview with Piers Haggard & Robert Wynne-Simmons
'Folk Music': New interview with Marc Wilkinson (Composer)
'Folk Sounds': New interview with Tony Dawe (Sound Mixer)
'Folk Art': New interview with Milly Burns (Set Dresser)
'Folk Tale': New interview with Simon Williams (Actor - Peter Edmonton)
'Return To Bix Bottom': Simon Williams returns to the ruins of old St. James Church

'The Ruins': New featurette about the setting of the *Blood on Satan's Claw*

'Touching The Devil: The Making of the *Blood on Satan's Claw*'

- Interview with director Piers Haggard

- Audio commentary with Piers Haggard, Robert Wynne-Simmons & Linda Hayden

- Audio commentary with Mark Gatiss, Jeremy Dyson & Reece Shearsmith

- Sleeve notes, Morris, M

Hamilton, J (2005) *Beasts in the cellar: the exploitation film career of Tony Tenser*, Godalming: Fab Press.

Hayden, L (2019), personal correspondence with the author.

Hill, C (1975) *The world turned upside down: radical ideas during the English Revolution*, London: Penguin.

Hoskins, W G (2005) *The making of the English landscape*, London: Hodder & Stoughton.

Hunt, L (1998), *British low culture: From safari suits to sexploitation*, London: Routledge.

Hunt, L (2002) 'Necromancy in the UK: witchcraft and the occult in British horror', in *British Horror Cinema* (eds Chibnall, Steve and Petley, Julian), London: Routledge.

Hunt, L (2008) *The League of Gentlemen*, Basingstoke: BFI/Palgrave Macmillan.

Hutchings, P (1993) *Hammer and Beyond: The British horror film*, Manchester: Manchester University Press.

Hutchings, P (2004) 'Uncanny landscapes in British film and television', *Visual Culture in Britain*, v5, n2.

Ingham, H D (2018) *We don't go back: A watcher's guide to folk horror*, Room 207 Press Watcher's Guides.

Jensen, P (1974) *Terence Fisher in conversation*, Little Shoppe of Horrors #21 quoted from Cooper, I (2016) *Frightmares: A history of British horror cinema*, Leighton Buzzard: Auteur.

Johnston, D (2017) *The sublime horror of the English countryside*, https://hcommons.org/deposits/item/hc:23929/ (accessed 6 July 2021).

Kristeva, J (1982) *Powers of horror: an essay on abjection*, translated by Leon S Roudiez, New York: Columbia University Press.

Krzywinska, T (2017) *Lurking beneath the skin: British pagan landscapes in popular cinema*, https://tanyakrzywinska.com/2017/01/31/lurking-beneath-the-skin-british-pagan-landscapes-in-popular-cinema/ (accessed 6 July 2020).

Legard, P (2015) *The Haunted Fields of England: Diabolical Landscapes and the Genii Locorum* in *Folk Horror Revival: Field Studies* (ed. Katherine Beem and Andy Paciorek), Wyrd Harvest Press.

Lowenthal, D (2015) *The past is a foreign country, revisited*, Cambridge: Cambridge University Press.

Lyons, K https://eofftvreview.wordpress.com/2018/05/02blood-on-satans-claw-1970/ Lyons, Kevin (accessed 7 September 2019).

Macfarlane, R (2015) 'The eeriness of the English countryside', The Guardian.

Monk, C and Sargeant, A (2002) *British Historical Cinema*, London: Routledge.

Murray, M (1921) *The Witch-cult in Western Europe*, Oxford: Oxford University Press.

Negarestani, R (2008) *Cyclonopedia, complicity with anonymous materials*, Melbourne: re.press.

Newland, P (2016) 'Folk horror and the contemporary cult of British rural landscape: the case of Blood on Satan's Claw', in *British Rural Landscape on Film*, (ed. Newland, P), Manchester: Manchester University Press.

Outram, D (2013) *The Enlightenment*, Cambridge: Cambridge University Press.

Payne, C (1994) *Toil and Plenty: Images of the Agricultural Landscape in England: 1780-1890*, Yale Centre for British Art, New Haven: Yale University Press.

Pevsner, N and Sherwood, J (1979, second edition) *The Buildings of England: Oxfordshire*, London: Penguin Books.

Porter, R (2002) *Enlightenment*, Basingstoke: Palgrave.

Reed, M (1997) *The Landscape of Britain*, London: Routledge.

Rigby, J (2015, fourth edition) *English Gothic: Classic horror cinema 1897-2015*, Cambridge: Signum Books.

Rosenthal, M (1982) *British Landscape Painting*, London: Phaidon.

Roymans, N (1995) 'The Cultural Biography of Urnfields and the long-term history of a mythical landscape', Archaeological Dialogues, Vol 2, Issue 1.

Sandbrook, D (2007), *White Heat: A history of Britain in the Swinging Sixties, 1964-70*, London: Abacus.

Scovell, A (2017), *Folk Horror: Hours dreadful and things strange*, Leighton Buzzard: Auteur.

Scovell A, *The evil under the soil*, https://folklorethursday.com/urban-folklore/the-evil-under-the-soil-burial-and-unearthing-in-folk-horror/ (accessed 7 June 2019).

Scovell, A https://celluloidwickerman.com/2014/07/17/the-music-of-folk-horror-part-6-blood-on-satans-claw/(accessed 7 June 2019).

Scovell, A https://celluloidwickerman.com/2014/08/04/the-music-of-folk-horror-part-7-musical-anachronisms/ (accessed 1 August 2019).

Sereny, G (1995) *The case of Mary Bell: A portrait of a child who murdered*, London: Pimlico.

Sharp, A (2015) 'Hell's Angel Blake - An annotated guide to a coven at Bix', in Folk Horror Revival: Field Studies (ed. Katherine Beem and Andy Paciorek), Wyrd Harvest Press

Short, C R (1991) *Imagined country: environment, culture and society*, London: Routledge.

Simpson, M J http://mjsimpson-films.blogspot.com/2013/11/interview-piers-haggard.html (accessed 24 April 2019).

Skempton, A, et al. (2002) *A Biographical Dictionary of Civil Engineers in Great Britain and Ireland: Vol 1: 1500 to 1830*, London: Thomas Telford.

Soar, K 'The bones of the land', (2019) Hellbore (issue 1).

Spencer, A (2010) 'Population of Birmingham'. *Bham.de*. (retrieved 6 November 2010).

Sweet, M (2015) *Black Aquarius*, BBC Sounds, https://www.bbc.co.uk/sounds/play/favourites/b05qvr63 (accessed 28 February 2020).

Taylor, D (1996) 'Don't overact with your fingers! The making of *Blood on Satan's Claw*', in *Shock: The essential guide to exploitation cinema*, Jaworzyn, Stefan (ed.), London: Titan Books.

Thomas, K (1978) *Religion and the decline of magic*, London: Penguin.

Tudor, A (1989) *Monsters and mad scientists: A cultural history of the horror movie*, Oxford: John Wylie & Sons.

Turner, A (2013, second edition) *Crisis? What crisis? Britain in the 1970s*, London Aurum Press.

Watson, T (2009) 'The Manson murders at 40', *Newsweek* New York.

Williams, S (2019), personal correspondence with the author.

Wylie, J (2007) *Landscape*, London: Routledge.

Wynne-Simmons, R http://www.robertwynne-simmons.co.uk/biog.html#anchor (accessed 1 December 2019).

Young, R (2010) 'The pattern under the plough', *Sight & Sound*, vol 20, issue 8.

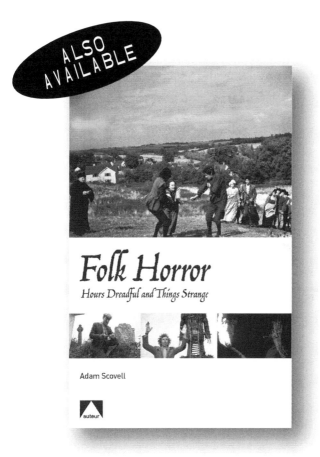

ALSO AVAILABLE

Folk Horror
Hours Dreadful and Things Strange

Adam Scovell

auteur

"Scovell...is a keen-eyed and enthusiastic curator, his tone perfectly pitched between that of the articulate academic and the box-set binger. He knows that folk horror provides succour as well as visceral thrills and draws clear links between topography, rurality and emerging hauntology theory." Ben Myers, New Statesman

"There has been very little scholarly work on folk horror, [and] Scovell does an admirable job of collecting this work. ...you won't find a more comprehensive introduction to folk-horror texts than Adam Scovell's Folk Horror: Hours Dreadful and Things Strange." Irish Journal of Gothic & Horror Studies

DEVIL'S ADVOCATES

"Auteur Publishing's new Devil's Advocates critiques on individual titles offer bracingly fresh perspectives from passionate writers. The series will perfectly complement the BFI archive volumes." Christopher Fowler, Independent on Sunday

THE COMPANY OF WOLVES – JAMES GRACEY

"Gracey does his part to add to the legacy of The Company of Wolves, strengthening the film's importance with a thoughtful monograph that is detailed and accessible, presenting arguments with deliberation and validity, never forcefully or self-righteous." Film Int.

THE WITCH – BRANDON GRAFIUS

The first stand-alone critical study of The Witch *provides the historical and religious background necessary for a fuller appreciation, including an insight into the Puritan movement in New England, as well as situating the film within a number of horror sub-genres (such as folk horror) as well as its other literary and folkloric influences.*

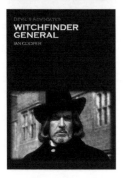

WITCHFINDER GENERAL – IAN COOPER

"I enjoyed it very much; it sets out all the various influences, both before and after the film, and indeed the essence of the film itself, very well indeed." Jonathan Rigby, author of English Gothic